D1208325

Fiberglass Rod Making

Fiberglass Rod Making

DALE CLEMENS

WINCHESTER PRESS

All photographs and drawings by the author.

Copyright © 1974 by Dale P. Clemens
All rights reserved

Library of Congress Catalog Card Number: 73–88879
ISBN: 0–87691–136–X

Fifth printing

WINCHESTER PRESS
205 East 42nd Street
New York, N.Y. 10017

To my children:

      ANNE —

her pride in me is always an inspiration, and

      BRIAN —

a great lover of nature and a most promising fisherman.

Acknowledgments

Very few things are ever accomplished alone by anyone. Certainly, I could never have written this book without the help and influence of many people. Foremost was my wife, Donna. Her encouragement and confidence overcame my inertia, and her understanding and patience with me was absolutely astounding.

One of the great custom-rod builders, Frank "Boots" Voigt, enthusiastically shared knowledge and techniques acquired over many years. Helpful market research was contributed by Jim Cabela. A certain letter of encouragement from Eric Leiser, "The Fireside Angler," arrived at a most crucial time. My secretary, Karen George, spent many extra hours typing and retyping the manuscript from my nearly illegible handwriting. A dear friend, Palmer Zigmund, gave me a needed hand with some of the photography, and Linda Brong shared ideas from her advertising experience. In addition to thanking all those mentioned by name, I want to express my appreciation to the staff at Winchester Press.

Contents

Introduction

For quite a few years I have been enjoying the pleasures and satisfactions of building custom fishing rods. My fishing interests have led me to travel quite a bit, and in the process I have met other custom builders and those who wanted to try their hand at it. There were many more of the latter, and while we all willingly shared our techniques and experience with those interested, there was no modern book on rod building listed anywhere.

As more and more people became interested, I found myself helping some of them secure blanks and other rod-building components from the various manufacturers and mail-order dealers. Ultimately, my hobby grew to a small part-time custom-tackle business. However, it became increasingly difficult to pass on the "how-to" information that so many people desired.

Then one day I was talking on the telephone with a large catalog dealer. He sells a very broad range of hunting, fishing, and camping gear, including the recent addition of an assortment of blanks and materials. He agreed that there was a great increase in custom rod building, as evidenced by his sales and the many requests for information his company received. Since he was not a rod builder, he found it very difficult to pass along to his customers any "how-to" information or advice. In fact, he said he was not even sure what items he should stock.

We both agreed that if there was some source of information on contemporary rod building to which an interested person could be referred, many reluctant people would get in on the fun of building their own rods. He then surprised me by asking, "Dale, why don't you write a book on the subject?" I muttered a startled reply about maybe a small pamphlet, but not a book. He encouraged me some more, and our conversation ended with my promise to at least give it some thought.

I finally got around to drawing up an outline of the specific subjects that I felt should be covered. It became apparent that it could not all be squeezed into a pamphlet, and a book was the only answer.

I contacted other catalog dealers and manufacturers to see if they thought a book was needed. The response was an overwhelming yes.

While I have built a great many rods of all kinds, it is not my vocation. My techniques have been essentially self-developed and evolved over a period of years. I could not overlook the fact that there may be better ways than my own of performing some of the operations. If I was to write a book, I felt I owed it to the reader to consult with a true full-time professional to make certain I was not missing something important.

There is a small group of professional custom-rod builders scattered across the country. Often found in the more famous fishing areas, these men are true masters of their craft. One of the most skillful of these men is Frank "Boots" Voigt, who operates Voigt's Custom Tackle in Islamorada, Florida—the fishing heart of the Florida Keys. Boots has spent his life working with fishing tackle, first in Maryland and now in the Keys. His biggest market is the large number of professional guides who operate in this fabulous fishing area. Consequently, his rods are in constant use and must stand up to the rigors of salt, sun, and big fish.

Fortunately, Boots is one of the sweetest guys around. In my preparation for this book he allowed me to spend a number of days with him in his shop, observing the techniques he has developed over the years. He willingly shared the secrets of his trade, and evenings often found us discussing the application of his experience to the home craftsman for whom this book is written. These evening talks were particularly enjoyable, since the discussion was always accompanied by his wife Daisy's homemade Key Lime Pie—she grows the limes right in their front yard.

Boots is also a great fisherman and licensed guide. When he can get away from his one-man shop, he is out testing his fly, spinning, and casting rods while seeking his clients' opinions. Many of his refinements and methods are found throughout this book. I felt the reader deserved this exposure to the exceptional professional to amplify my own experience.

It is my sincere wish, then, that in these pages you will find ideas and techniques which will enable you to advance in the exciting hobby, or perhaps even vocation, of custom-rod building. I know of no greater satisfaction for the dedicated fisherman.

—Dale P. Clemens
Allentown, Pa.

Fiberglass Rod Making

1. Why Build Your Own?

Perhaps you have wanted to try your hand at rod building for some time and have just been waiting for a little guidance on how to start. On the other hand, you may be still quite skeptical about making your own rod, either because you question your ability to do so, or because you are not convinced it is worth doing. "After all," you might say, "aren't there plenty of good rods available from manufacturers?" To which I would have to answer, "Yes, but . . . "

It is that "Yes, but . . . " response that I would like to explore a bit with you. I have been custom-building rods for quite a few years now. Since it has been a great source of pleasure and enjoyment to me, I would like to share with you some of the reasons why I and an increasing number of others are building their own rods.

First off, no one will put the care and attention into a rod that you will, when you are building the rod for yourself. Despite the advantages of mass production, a great amount of the important detail that relates to performance must still be done by hand. Consider the alignment of the rod to determine precisely on which side of the blank the guides and fixed reel seat (if one is used) are placed. There are 360° around a blank, but only one spot is the correct one! And no two, or two thousand, blanks made from the same mandrel will bend exactly the same, because of many uncontrollable variables in manufacturing. This means that the perfect spacing of guides, for optimum performance, will vary on blanks from within a production run. Testing to determine spacing requires simply too much time and labor for the manufacturer to even consider doing it for each individual rod when he must turn out thousands. Instead, the average spacing is determined and all the people in the winding room use those figures.

Add to the above problems the human element of workers. On some days they feel good—their mind is on their work, and they perform as expected. On others, it is a different story, as we all know. It has been rumored that in Detroit, people in the know try to buy cars built on days other than Mondays or Fridays. I do not know if that is true, but it certainly illustrates the problem of the human element in mass production. Some manufacturers train their workers well and try to exercise quality control to achieve consistency. Obviously, that cost is passed along to you. However, all of the above points still apply in varying degrees, and you're not getting what you, and you alone, can build into a rod.

Fittings, their number and quality, are yet another matter. A corner cut here, a compromise made there, can do wonders to keep production costs down. From the manufacturer's viewpoint, rods are made to be sold. Sure, they have to perform reasonably well on the average, but they must be sold in sufficient quantity to make a profit. Therefore, "eye appeal," as dictated by the market-research findings of the advertising departments and sales departments, often wins out in determining just what does go into the product.

Good manufacturers try their best. However, as stated initially, you cannot expect anyone to put the care and attention to detail into a rod that you will put in. The proof is found in building a few of your own rods and fishing them. You will see that the very best can only be achieved by custom-building your own rods. The very best of quality is synonymous with custom craftsmanship.

Proceeding on to other areas, I am sure you have your own preferences in the action, balance, feel, and weight of a fishing rod. You know exactly the range of weights you intend to cast with a given rod. For reasons such as your physical build, or the conditions under which you fish, a certain length rod is ideal. One of my big pleasures is tarpon fishing in the Caribbean, and I go there whenever I can. The kind of rod designed specifically for this kind of fishing simply is not available in Allentown, Pennsylvania, where I live. I could take my chances and order a rod from a catalog, but I have learned the hard way just how ambiguous catalog descriptions can be. Really, the only way for me to get *exactly* the rod I want is to build it myself.

If you have ever found yourself saying, "I wish I could find a rod that . . . " you are a prime candidate to become a rod builder. Perhaps you are a utilitarian who says, "To hell with the fancy appearance. I want a straightforward, simple-looking, but top-quality rod which will . . . " Again, the best route is to do it yourself. The same principle applies if you love the beauty of unique design and careful craftsmanship. Sit down and think a bit about exactly what you want in a fishing rod. Chances are you will come to the conclusion that the best way to get it is to design and build it yourself.

The real thrill of fishing comes from outwitting the fish. It is something that you and you alone do. It is a conquest of one man over one of nature's worthy opponents. The point here is the "oneness" — you do it yourself. Many a fisherman has learned that his fishing thrill is enhanced when the fish is conquered on a fly that he tied. It is much better than on a fly he bought. Capturing your fish with a rod that you alone made provides an even greater thrill.

Besides being outdoors, the pleasure of fishing comes from the handling and mastery of your equipment: the comfortable feel of the rod in your hand and the rhythm of the cast, be it with a 10-foot stick in heavy surf or a delicate midge rod on a remote stream. How much more enjoyable when you have built the rod, one of the very sources of your pleasure.

Fishing is, unfortunately, a seasonal thing. Unless you have both unlimited funds and time, you cannot chase the fishing seasons around the globe. For many fishermen, a great part of the year is spent reminiscing back to last season and contemplating the one ahead. An increasing number have found that "tackle tinkering" is a wonderful way to extend their enjoyment of fishing beyond the regular season. Rod building is "tackle tinkering" in its finest, most constructive form. I, for one, have a great love for fishing. Over the years I refused to be confined by the fishing season. First I took up fly tying and then rod building. Next, I branched into amateur fish taxidermy. And now — of all things — I am writing a book about rod building. I know how much richer is my total "fishing" experience than the poor guy who only gets to fish during the season.

It is certainly not shameful to be proud of a fond possession no matter how expensive or inexpensive it may be. People have spent fortunes in seeking to own the truly unique, the one of its kind, be it an object of art or utility. A friend of mine has an extensive collection of antique surveying instruments. His most prized possession is one that was the only model of its kind ever made—and that is why it is so valuable to him; it is unique. Why shouldn't we, as fishermen, feel equal pride in an exclusive rod of our own creation? It will be the only one of its kind.

A long-range project of mine has been to put together a collection of different kinds of rods for the different kinds of fishing I enjoy. Each rod was to serve a specific purpose: trout fly, bonefish fly, freshwater spinning, etc. But each rod, in style, color, trim, and finish, was to be like the others, yet unmistakably custom-made. Part of this bevy of unique rods was responsible for one of the nicest fishing experiences I ever had. Three of the rods, my bonefish fly rod, tarpon fly rod, and tarpon spinning rod, were temporarily left leaning against a dockside wall while I gathered up other gear at the completion of a day's fishing in the Florida Keys. When I turned to get the rods, I met a vaguely familiar-looking fellow admiring them. He asked who made the rods for me and a conversation followed. All of a sudden I knew why he looked familiar; he was the late Joe Brooks, certainly one of the finest and most talented fishing gentlemen of all times. I had read his books and recognized his picture. We shared a couple of beers and some more conversation, and ended up fishing together the next day. It was a great opportunity to get to know this exceptional man—and it never would have happened if it had not been for the rods I had built. Perhaps your "conversational pieces" will lead to all kinds of exciting experiences.

If you want to buy a truly top-quality rod with the best of hardware and most careful construction, it is going to be expensive—and you're still not certain of what you will get. You can make a rod of better quality for a lot less money. If you are the pure utilitarian and want the best-quality materials, but without the frills and fancy trim associated with top-quality rods, you are going to have a hard time finding one to buy. The utilitarian rods made commercially are usually the cheap rods made with cheap materials and poor workmanship. In that case you can build your kind of quality into as straightforward and simple a design as you want, and spend no more money in doing it. To build your rod of the very best materials will not be cheap. However, you will thereafter have the best obtainable, which, when performance and durability are considered, is true economy. When you compare the cost to the most expensive rods available, you will find that you have invested considerably less money. If your budget does not permit you to buy the best of materials, you will still have a better rod (because of your careful construction) at less outlay than a middle-priced, mass-produced rod. What I am saying here is that you definitely can save money in building your own, since labor costs are one of the biggest items to the manufacturer. To get an accurate picture of your savings you must compare your rod to commercial rods of comparable quality.

One of the most rewarding experiences in custom-rod building is designing and making a rod for a gift. To another fisherman, I can think of few gifts that are as much appreciated as a rod custom-crafted for him alone. The whole essence and spirit of giving is portrayed in a gift such as this. It says you really care, you wanted to give something of yourself. A very close business associate of mine was transferred across the country. We had enjoyed some memorable fishing trips together, yet because of our business relationship, it had always been difficult to really express the personal closeness I felt for this man. In my parting gift of a custom rod, I feel I was able to convey a bit of how I felt, and judging from his reaction I believe it was communicated. In another instance, a Florida friend generously lent me the use of his 16-foot Boston Whaler for a week's family vacation there. I knew he would never accept an offer of payment, so when I returned I built a fly rod for his thirteen-year-old son. The boy was eager to try fly fishing and was awed by a custom-built rod with his name on it. I think my friend realized how much I appreciated his lending me his boat. Perhaps the carefully crafted rod you build for your own son — a labor of love — will help you bridge the generation gap. Long after you are gone it may be a prized possession that your son proudly explains to a friend: "My dad built this rod for me." Who of us would not like to have a rod like that in remembrance of our father?

Some of us like to use hobbies and spare time to augment our incomes where possible. Custom-made fishing rods are a natural. The profits can help finance our fishing ventures. A hunter friend of mine has done this with taxidermy. He loves the work, is in great demand, and, as a consequence, is able to afford exotic hunting trips, which before he would have denied himself. Markets for custom rods are everywhere: angling friends, members of sportsmen's clubs, and your local tackle dealer. Most dealers would like to have a few top-quality

Two custom spinning rods. The upper rod is 7 feet long and has butt hosel and trim ring of walnut faced with white plastic. The reel seat has a walnut insert. The lower rod, a very light 6-footer, also has walnut and white plastic hosels, and the reel seat insert is made of rings of walnut and popular.

A 9-foot fly rod with double-locking sliding-hood reel seat and plastic hosel.

A very light 7-foot spinning rod with sliding reel seat. The shaped butt plate and small winding check in front of the grip are made of plastic.

A 6-foot-9-inch spinning rod with hosels made of black plastic inlaid with very thin white plastic. Butt trim is black-and-white "corkscrew wrap," and guide wraps are black over silver Mylar. Reel seat is black with chrome hardware.

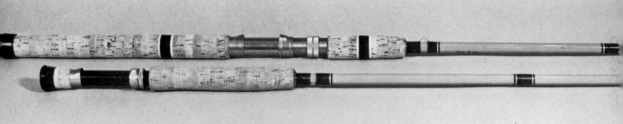

At top, a two-handed 8-foot spinning rod. Trim rings are walnut faced with white plastic, and butt cap is a shortened leg cap for tubular metal furniture. Below, a 9-foot fly rod with short detachable fighting butt.

A surf spinning rod with rubber butt cap made from a furniture-leg cap and a white plastic hosel on the foregrip. Guide wraps are red open spirals over white underwrap.

custom rods for the customer who desires something unique. If the dealer will not invest in a few for his inventory, he may be interested in carrying a sample of your work and selling a custom-rod-building service for a percentage of the sales price. If you decide on doing this, don't make the mistake of underpricing your rods. The man who wants a custom rod expects it to be expensive. Put your price at least as high as the very best rods available commercially. They are good, but you have the advantage of uniqueness, which the right customer will gladly pay for. Have a conference with your customer beforehand. Determine what he wants in *all* respects, including style and color of trim. In the process you will appear to be quite the expert; you will educate him, and he will be happier with the rod.

If, in this discussion, I have touched upon some of your motivations and desires, do not be put off for fear that it is too difficult a task. Some years back I developed a hankering to build my own rod. I contacted a catalog dealer who sold supplies, but mainly pushed "rod-building kits," blanks with handles installed on which you only had to wrap the guides. The kits were quite expensive, compared with the purchase of the necessary components alone, and I had a very limited budget at the time. I explained that I had no experience and he seized upon the opportunity to extol the advantages of his kits. In the process, he incorrectly informed me that building a rod from scratch was very difficult and he made all the fitting jobs sound horrendous. As a result, I did not build a rod from scratch or from one of his kits. That fellow set me back over a year. I still had the hankering, but I was afraid I just could not handle the job of building from scratch. Finally, I mustered the courage and took the plunge. And, lo and behold, it wasn't very difficult. In fact, on even my first rod, I found it relatively easy and a great amount of fun. When I caught my first fish on that rod it was I who was really hooked, and I have been at it in earnest ever since.

Lest at this point you get the opinion that I am one of those enviable "naturals" when it comes to handling tools, let me quickly dispel the notion. I really view myself as all thumbs in this category. I have always been rather fearful of things mechanical, and while I have acquired a few used woodworking tools, I must confess that my main product has been sawdust. I am reluctant to tackle even minor household repairs and my wife must be constantly after me to fix this or that.

In more cases than not, she has given up, and in desperation hired a repairman. So, if I, who am an absolute bumbler with tools, can build custom fishing rods, I am sure that you—armed with what I have learned over the years and put into this book—can quickly master the art of rod building. In so doing, I know you will expand your "fishing" horizons greatly and derive an even greater pleasure from your time on the water.

2. Selection of the Blank

There are quite a few components that go into the building of a fishing rod, but the blank is certainly the primary one. More than anything else, the selection of the blank will determine the characteristics of the rod. I am not going to go into a discourse on the relative merits of different materials from which a blank can be made. Instead, let me simply say that with all the tremendous advances in technology and design that have occurred, modern, quality, hollow fiberglass is the best material from which to make a fishing rod.

In the manufacture of quality glass blanks, a special glass cloth made of fine, thin unidirectional strands is used. This glass cloth is woven so that there are many more strands running the length of the rod than run around the rod. If you look closely at a top-knotch rod you can see this. The glass cloth is chrome-treated and wrapped around a steel rod or mandrel. Next, it is impregnated with special resins and wrapped with cellophane to provide high-pressure lamination while it is cured with heat. After curing, the cellophane is removed and the blank is sanded and treated with another resin to seal the surface, providing a smooth glass-like finish.

The quality blank of today is the end product of an enormous amount of expensive research into materials and techniques. You and I are the beneficiaries of that research. We have available to us at modest cost (thanks to economies of large-scale production) the best blanks ever made for fishing rods.

This research and continual improvement is an ongoing process.

The blanks available now are greatly superior to those of five or ten years ago, and we can look forward to even better blanks in the future. For example, two new interesting fiber materials currently being test-marketed by a number of companies are boron and graphite. The latter seems to have the most promising characteristics, but only time in use will tell. The graphite fibers are made into a blank using an epoxy laminate system much like the normal fiberglass manufacturing process. The prime characteristic is the increased stiffness per unit of weight. This property enables a blank of a given action to be made that will weigh only about two-thirds as much as fiberglass, and about half as much as bamboo.

When a bare graphite blank is handled, it seems, and is, considerably stiffer than a comparable bare fiberglass blank. However, the blank loads well from the weight of a fly line or lure. It is, therefore, more difficult to judge the action of the blank or completed rod unless you actually cast with it. Some of the testers feel that a graphite fly rod will be capable of casting a tighter loop and picking up more line from the water. In any event, it is just another one of many examples where research has provided and is continuing to provide the best blanks ever devised for fishing rods.

When you set out to build a custom rod, you have a specific purpose in mind for that rod. I am not referring here to the type — that is, fly, spinning, casting, or trolling — but rather to the use to which you intend to put the rod. Perhaps it is to cast very light lures on a small trout stream, or it might be for casting a heavy fly line long distances on the bonefish flats. Whatever the use, it is specific and you need just the right blank. So the very important first step is the selection of that blank.

Be wary here, or you can easily become confused. For example, fly rods can be described as being dry-fly action, trout action, bass-steelhead action, salmon action, saltwater-flats action, and general saltwater action. While these descriptive terms are helpful to the novice in selecting a rod, much more precise information is needed by you, the custom builder. One of the decided advantages of building a rod is that in the process you will become much more knowledgeable about fishing rods and how they function. Not only will this enable you to make or select a rod better suited to your needs, but it will increase your appreciation of and pleasure in the sport.

In order to start with the proper blank, you need to understand some of the basics of the theory of rod action. We don't need to get very technical here, so let's jump in. The purpose of a fishing rod with which we cast is to amplify muscle power along a shaft in order to propel a weight. The length of the shaft or rod provides us with a lever. The flexing of the rod during the cast collects and temporarily stores part of the amplified muscle energy. Then, when the rod subsequently straightens, or recoils, the stored energy is released and is applied to propel a weight — the lure, bait, or fly line. Therefore, the main function of the rod is to bend and recoil. This flexing must be "in time" with our casting rhythm, and we must be able to feel the bending and recoil occurring during the cast so that we know at what precise point to release the line.

The blank manufacturer determines over what length or what portion of the rod this bending takes place. The greater the length of rod that bends, the longer it takes to recoil or straighten. On the other hand, the shorter the length that bends, the faster it recoils. For this reason rod action is described in terms of speed — the speed with which the rod bends and recoils. The terms generally used to describe rod action are: extra fast (where just the very tip or upper quarter bends), fast (the upper third bends), moderate or medium (approximately the upper half), and slow (progressive curve increases from butt to tip). This can be seen graphically in the accompanying diagram.

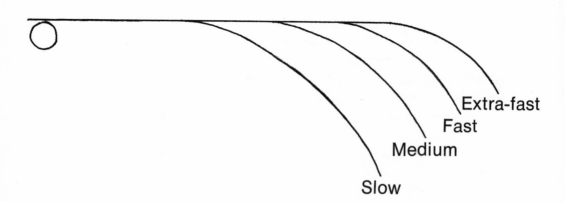

We should realize here that these definitions of speed also end up referring to the speed necessary in the timing of our casting. The extra-fast-action rod, for example, allows us very little time to feel the flex of the rod and to judge the instant of line release. There is practically no "feel" in this type of rod, since everything happens too quickly. Casting becomes quick and jerky instead of smooth and graceful. A lot of the enjoyment is lost. More muscle power is required as well. A slower action, on the other hand, permits the rod to do most of the work of casting for us.

In building a rod you can exercise some degree of further refinement over this action, as we will see, but your initial job is to select the proper rod action and length for the specific job you want the rod to perform. Most of you, I am sure, already have an idea of the action you desire in a particular rod. Perhaps it is that of an old favorite or one belonging to a friend, or a rod in the dealer's rack. Using a simple test, you can identify the action of any rod.

Hold the grip firmly in both hands at about the level of your belt, with the rod pointing directly away from you. The tip should be about the same height as the grip from the ground. Hold the grip rigid and wave the tip of the rod back and forth parallel to the ground. As the rod bends, you can look along it and see the action. It is an easy matter to see how far down from the tip of the rod the bend extends, and therefore how "slow" or "fast" the action is.

To determine the action of a blank or rod, hold the butt rigid with both hands and wave the tip back and forth parallel to the ground.

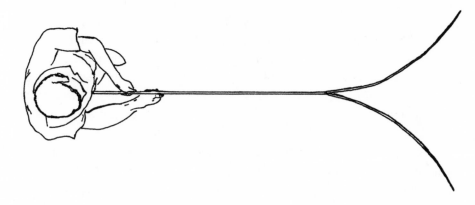

Types of rod action have changed as fishing styles evolved. Many years ago when rods were mostly fly rods and made of bamboo, their principal use was for fishing wet flies. The desired action was quite slow and the rods flexed all the way down into the cork grips. With the advent of dry-fly fishing, the buggy-whip action of the standard wet-fly rod gave way, of necessity, to a faster action with the bending more confined to the tip. When spinning was first imported to this country the rods were of medium action. However, as the popularity of fishing grew and as bamboo was replaced by glass, the manufacturers new to spinning turned out rods that were more and more tip-action rods. The term "fast taper" came into vogue. There was a tremendous influx of both fishermen and manufacturers new to the sport. The manufacturers, eager to provide what the public wanted and thus sell their wares, produced ever more extra-fast-action rods for spinning, fly fishing, and casting. At best, most of these rods were difficult to cast. The short bend and recoil occurred so rapidly that it required ultra-split-second timing to release the line at the correct instant. Also, more effort had to be expended and much of the pleasure was lost. Unfortunately, many fishermen were new to the sport; they had never experienced the joy and ease of casting with a slower-action rod.

In recent years, bamboo became increasingly scarce, and more and more expensive to manufacture into rods. At the same time new developments and techniques in glass made it possible to build rods surpassing bamboo in quality and performance. Today more experienced manufacturers, prompted by now more experienced fishermen, are turning away from the stiff tip-action rods to the more moderate actions. As a result, we are beginning to have available a wider range of blanks. Hopefully, each year we will see a greater number of slower-action blanks and rods on the market. I suggest that if you are undecided between two given blanks, and other things are equal, you will always do well to select the one with the slower action, be it for fly, spinning, or casting. I would also recommend choosing "regular taper" over "fast taper." Even after having made such a selection, you may want to incorporate into the building of the rod techniques which will slow the action even more.

Another factor in selecting the proper blank for the rod you have in mind is the weight, or range of weights, it is designed to cast. Referring again to rod action, or the portion of the rod that bends or flexes,

will have to be short. With it, you plan to cast a very light weight, and the only way that can be accomplished is if a sizable length of rod bends and recoils. Now, if you need a sizable length of rod to bend, and you have only a short rod, it becomes necessary for practically the entire rod to bend. So on this type of rod you need a slow action; it must flex all the way down into the grip.

Now, let us assume you want to cast the same light weight a greater distance on large, open water. In this case the manufacturer can add length to the butt end of essentially the same rod as above. This extra length gives you more leverage and you are able to cast farther.

One day while fly fishing for tarpon in the Florida Keys, I was with a friend who was using an 8-foot fly rod. The actual bend of his rod (not percentage of the rod, but the number of inches that bent) was the same as mine. However, I was using a 9-foot rod. Both rods cast a weight-forward #10 line, but mine cast farther with the same effort. As is often the case in this kind of fishing, we had to cast out a good distance to reach the fish as they cruised by on the flats. My rod, due to its extra length in the butt end, was much more capable of doing this. I suggested to my companion that he try my rod. After just a few casts he was attaining the same distance as I had been. The point is that the length of the rod, as well as the action, must fit the job at hand. Other things being equal, a longer rod will usually cast farther with less effort.

The height and build of the fisherman have some effect on the choice of rod length. The shorter fellow will find it more difficult to cast a very long rod. This seems especially pronounced with heavier fly rods. I am on the short side (5 feet 7 inches) and it took me some time to master the previously mentioned 9-foot fly rod for tarpon fishing. That length is definitely my upper limit, and even then, I must admit that I am more comfortable with an 8½-foot rod. So, in selecting a blank for length, give some thought to who is going to fish the rod.

One of the tricks of the professionals is to purchase long blanks—often 9 feet—of the general type of taper they desire and then to cut various lengths from the long blank to make up different rods having different actions and purposes. For example, a 9-foot blank might have 18 inches removed from the butt end and 6 inches cut off the tip to provide a blank for a medium-action 7-foot spinning rod. The same blank could have 1 foot removed from the butt and become an 8-foot fly rod, and so on. There is no doubt that this technique works, but it requires great experience in judging and predicting the actions of a blank. As such, it will be of little use for the hobbyist unless he has built enough rods to gain the necessary judgment of blanks. A willingness to experiment, however, will allow you to modify the action of a given blank by a small amount of judicious pruning.

If you follow the previous suggestions, you should be very capable of selecting the blank you need. The question sometimes arises about "taper" and how this should affect your choice. Most catalogs will list some pertinent facts regarding the taper: butt size (often given in 100ths of an inch), mid-size (most often in 64ths), and tip size (just about always in 64ths). They might also list the rod as "regular taper" or "fast taper" as mentioned earlier. A little reflection will indicate that these merely support what we previously discussed as rod action—what portion of the rod bends, and the weight it is designed to cast. A rod that tapers down only near the tip will have a fast action when compared to one that tapers from the butt. Of two blanks the same length and taper, the one that has the smaller diameter overall will cast a lighter weight. The vital statistics of taper have a purpose, but it is generally not to describe rod action or the weight to be cast. Instead they provide the very necessary information we need to order the proper fittings for the rod we are building. These would include tip size, reel seat and reel-seat bushings, cork-ring sizes or grips, and ferrules if the blank does not have the ferrules installed.

The most recent development in fiberglass rods has been the so called "non-ferrule" connection or glass-to-glass ferrule. This design was first introduced by some of the best manufacturers and has gained so much popularity that most companies have begun to utilize it in their top-of-the-line rods. While it has some advantages, it has disadvantages too, and I feel the value of the glass-to-glass ferrule has been exaggerated. This is attributable to the naturally competitive efforts of companies to come up with innovations which will sell more of their products. Such competition is highly desirable, for it provides us with increasingly better equipment. Sometimes, however, an advertising campaign is so successful that a certain feature receives enough attention to catapult it into the gimmick category. It becomes the vogue and everybody has to have it. Few people, then, consider the relative merits of the feature. We saw this happen in the past with extra-fast-action rods and fast-taper designs.

More quality rod blanks with glass ferrules are becoming available. However, there are still many unferruled, and aluminum-alloy ferruled, blanks offered. You may not be able to find exactly the blank you want with a glass ferrule. My concern is that you do not, therefore, forego the pleasure and many advantages of building your own because you feel you would end up with an inferior piece of equipment or an "old-fashioned" rod. Rods made with the newest metal ferrules are just as good as the glass-ferruled rods, and lack some of the disadvantages.

To understand this aspect of rod construction more fully, we need to examine the history and function of the ferrule. The ideal rod would be of one piece its entire length, so as to fully preserve the smooth bending and action. However, because of the practical considerations of storage and transportation, this is generally ruled out. We need a rod that will break down into two or more sections, which necessitates some kind of slip joint. For years this joint was accomplished with a metal ferrule. On quality bamboo rods, it was always made of nickel silver. This is an alloy consisting of 18 percent nickel, 12–18 percent zinc, and the balance copper. It does not fatigue easily, has high tensile strength, and is reasonably light in weight.

A lesser-quality ferrule was frequently used on many earlier glass production rods. It was nickel-plated brass, cheaper and heavier, and definitely had both limited strength and life.

In recent years an exciting new metal ferrule has appeared. Anodized aluminum alloys are now used by Featherweight Products to make a ferrule that is 300 percent lighter and 25 percent stronger than nickel-plated brass. These are machined with a silken-smooth cushion fit made possible by a slight taper on the male and female pieces, and utilize a replaceable rubber O-ring on the slide (male piece). They are lighter than, and compare quite favorably with, the more expensive nickel-silver ferrules. If the rod is to be used in salt water, they are preferable by far, since nickel silver is extremely vulnerable to corrosion in salt water.

Shorter metal ferrules of all three metals have been introduced. These are often called "mini-ferrules" or "micro-ferrules." Their shorter length reduces the flat spot somewhat, but only at the price of reduced strength. As a result their use is confined to very light rods for delicate fishing.

In an attempt to utilize the flexibility and strength of fiberglass itself, a ferrule was developed which used a metal plug permanently affixed within the tube of one rod section. The open tube of the blank of the other rod section slipped over this metal plug, which was built with a taper to perfectly match the tube into which it fit. This is the metal-to-glass ferrule still in much use. However, as in all ferrule joints using the fiberglass tube of the blank, the walls had to be reinforced in some way or they would split under heavy bending pressure. This reinforcement is accomplished with either extra glass around the walls of the joint or a double layer of thread wrapping.

Instead of a metal plug, if one of solid fiberglass is used, an entirely glass-to-glass joint results. All other aspects of this ferrule are the same as the metal-to-glass ferrule.

Two additional glass ferrules were developed. One utilizes a fiberglass sleeve which has one half glued over the tip section of the blank, forming a glass socket or female ferrule. The forward end of the butt section of the blank becomes the male ferrule, which slides into the sleeve. The other type of glass-to-glass joint must be manufactured on two separate mandrels, one for each section of the blank. This obviously increases the cost of this type of rod. The design consists of a tip section whose lower end terminates in a large enough diameter to allow it to slip over the forward end of the butt section. In effect, the lower end becomes a female ferrule.

If we are going to get this ferrule question in proper perspective, we must realize that regardless of the material used — metal, metal to glass, or glass to glass — there is always a more rigid section involved. In the case of glass, it may be a solid glass plug on the double walls where hollow glass fits over hollow glass. *Any* ferrule results in more rigidity at the joint.

The proponents of glass-to-glass connections will claim that solid fiberglass plugs and reinforced fiberglass walls will flex better than metal. Even over the few short inches occupied by the ferrule, I suppose that if some kind of delicate scientific test were run, this could be proved — but I do not think it really matters a bit when it gets down to the practicability of actual casting. There are other advantages and disadvantages of glass-to-glass ferrules, but in all honesty I do not think casting is really one of them. In fact, a well-known consumer testing service just recently tested 35 different makes of fiberglass fly rods which included all of the previously described types of ferrules. When it came down to any relationship that might exist between ferrule design and performance in casting, they could draw no conclusions based on their tests. All cast equally well.

The primary merits of a glass connection are that it makes a neat, hardly noticeable joint, and is lighter than plated brass or nickel silver. The latter advantage of weight saving at the ferrule can alter the balance of the rod and give it a different "feel" in the hand of the caster. However, there is little noticeable weight saving over the new (anodized-aluminum-alloy) ferrules. The tapered fiberglass-to-fiberglass ferrule and the aluminum ferrule with O-ring are both easier to use and more resistant to dirt fouling than the other ferrules.

There are some disadvantages of glass ferrules that the advertising people do not talk about. For one thing, the joint tends to loosen sooner than metal and no longer provides a tight fit. Unfortunately, when that happens there is little that can be done about it. Metal ferrule joints can also loosen in time, but the ferrule itself is easily replaced. An aluminum-alloy ferrule with rubber O-ring can often be restored to a tight fit merely by replacing the O-ring. With a glass connection you face a serious problem if one section of the glass ferrule splits, or becomes cracked or broken. Since the female or tube end is the most vulnerable, it is generally placed on the tip section. So, a broken glass ferrule means replacing the entire tip section of the rod—assuming a replacement is still available.

The custom-rod builder can make a glass-to-glass ferrule of the solid-plug type if he desires. This is covered in the chapter on construction details. In my opinion, appearance is the main advantage. Overall, I feel the anodized-aluminum-alloy ferrule with the rubber O-ring really is as good a choice. The decision is yours—after all, that is what "custom" rod building is all about.

3. Tools,
Materials, and Components

In setting out to build a rod, the selection of the blank is, of course, only the first step. There are various other materials and components that you will need. Unless you understand their uses, it can be rather bewildering leafing through a catalog. You will also want to know what constitutes quality in a given component.

Before discussing these materials, it will be helpful to understand the basic assembly of each of the different types of rods. You will then be better able to visualize where each of the parts is used.

Fishing rods consist of only four basic parts: the blank, the handle or grip, the reel seat, and the guides. In some types of rods, a preassembled handle, which includes the reel seat, is used. Briefly, in word and diagram, here is how each of the different types of rods is assembled.

CASTING AND SPIN-CAST RODS

This is the easiest type of rod to build, since the blank (A) is simply mounted with a butt ferrule. The ferrule (B) must have the proper diameter for the blank and the proper size male plug (C) to fit into the handle (D) you have selected. All that remains is to wrap on the guides and tip-top.

Assembly of casting and spin-casting rods.

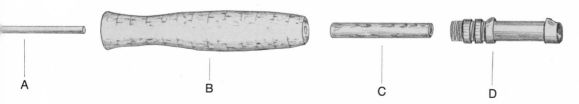

Assembly of a fly rod.

FLY RODS

The reel seat is mounted on the extreme butt end of the rod, over a wood bushing used to fill the space between the blank and the reel seat. The bushing (C) is glued to the blank (A), and the reel seat (D), in turn, is glued to the bushing. Immediately ahead of the reel seat are glued either cork rings from which a grip is shaped, or a pre-constructed shaped grip (B). To finish off the appearance of the grip, a winding check is glued to the front end of the grip. The above steps are performed in the order given. (If the ferrules have not been factory-installed, they are glued on prior to the above steps.) Finally, the hook-keeper, guides, and tip-top are attached.

SPINNING RODS

If the ferrules are not factory-installed, they are glued to the blank in the position desired. The work then progresses from butt toward the tip. First, the cork rings, from which the rear grip is fashioned, are glued to the extreme butt end of the blank (A) and to each other. Or a preconstructed rear grip (E) is used. The butt cap is glued to the rear end of this grip. Next, the bushings (C) for the reel seat are glued in place on the blank ahead of the rear grip, and the reel seat (D) is glued

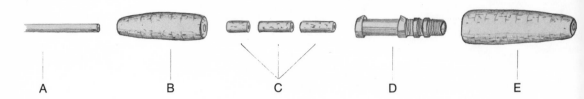

A   B   C   D   E

Assembly of a spinning rod.

over top of the bushings. Cork rings for fashioning the foregrip are glued to the blank and to each other, or a preconstructed foregrip (B) is used. If a rod hosel is to be included in the design, it is glued to the blank ahead of the foregrip, or a winding check is glued to the front of the foregrip for protective trim. The hookkeeper, guides, and tip-top are affixed last.

TROLLING OR BOAT RODS

Progressing again from butt toward the tip, the gimbal or butt cap (G) is glued to the end of the long wooden handle (F). The reel seat (D) is then glued in place on the forward end of the handle (E), using a bushing, if necessary, to make a tight fit. This completes the separate handle assembly. (Some surf rods are made with similar handle assemblies.) Next, the male ferrule (C) that slides into the open ferrule end of the reel seat is glued to the rear of the foregrip (B). Once again, a bushing may be needed for a tight fit. The butt end of the blank (A) is glued into the forward end of the foregrip, which has been drilled and shaped to accept and hold the butt firmly. The proper guides are then wrapped onto the blank and the tip-top attached.

Assembly of trolling and boat rods.

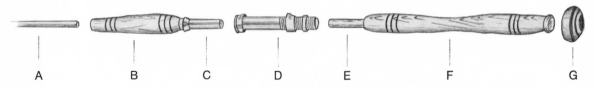

A   B   C   D   E   F   G

As you can see, the assembly of a fishing rod is really a rather simple affair. If approached with care and a little patience, just about anyone should be able to turn out a fine rod.

TOOLS

There is no need for any special or complicated tools. The chances are good that you already have what you need. I have first listed those that are basic to the construction of any rod. They are surprisingly few and simple. Yet using them alone, you can build a great rod with an appearance of which you can be justly proud.

Round file, about 10 inches long and ¼ inch at the largest diameter, with medium-fine teeth. It is used to remove material from the inside of bushings, preassembled cork grips, or cork rings to fit the taper of the blank.

Wood dowels, short sections about 6–7 inches long and of ¼-inch and ⅜-inch diameters. Wrapped with coarse sandpaper, they can be used instead of round files; or wrapped with fine sandpaper, they do an excellent job of fine-finishing the inside diameters of bushings, grips, and cork rings.

Sandpaper, a general assortment of coarse, medium, and fine for use with dowels or for shaping cork grips. Also used to dress the feet of guides.

Pipe cleaners, the best thing I have found for applying glue to blanks and the insides of bushings, reel seats, grips, and rings.

Masking tape, to hold guides in place while their position is checked and while wrapping them to the blank.

Razor blade or X-Acto knife, for cutting the wrapping thread close to the completed wrap.

India ink and pen, for the final touch of signing the completed rod.

TOOLS FOR FANCY TRIM

Something in my nature seems to make me constantly search for new and easier ways to do things. When I first started building rods, I looked with envy at some of the fancy trim built into the handle assemblies of expensive commercial rods. "Wow," I thought, "if I had lathes, drill presses, and other expensive power tools, I could incorporate some of those ideas into my own rods." Since I did not have that kind of equipment, that something in my nature took over. After a lot of trial and error I came up with far simpler and a lot less costly methods for duplicating the fancy trim. I will go into the techniques in the section on construction details, but let me list the additional tools you will need if you decide you want to try this.

Electric hand drill, my power supply for turning and cutting functions.

Hole saw, preferably the type that has a drill bit (usually ¼-inch) in the center and various-size round saw blades that fit into grooves in the base plate.

Arbor, to fit the drill. While these can be purchased separately, you can use one from a rubber sanding disc or from a buffing wheel made for use in an electric hand drill.

That's it! You probably already have the drill or can borrow one. It is amazing what you can do with these three tools. Rings of various length can be cut out of wood or plastic using the hole saw. The rings can be glued together in various combinations and installed on the arbor for shaping tapers and finishing. Using this technique, you can make decorative trim rings for insertion into the grip, or rod hosels and butt plates for the ends of the grips. By temporarily attaching cork rings to a dowel, you can chuck the dowel into the drill and shape your own grips by turning. You can do all these things, and more, and you do not need a lot of expensive, complicated equipment.

CONSTRUCTION MATERIALS

Ferrule cement is a thermoplastic cement used mainly for cementing ferrules and tip to the blank. It is set by the application of heat to the joint, providing a quick bond. Its main advantage is that the reapplication of heat allows rapid removal of parts for replacement, or for realignment. The primary disadvantage is that the bond is not as strong or permanent as possible with the modern adhesives such as Pliobond. Personally, I feel the advantages make it worth using on ferrules and tip-tops. A number of different formulations are available with the older wax-resin base (generally in stick form); these are not as good as the newer vinyl formulas (generally in liquid form).

Liquid glue is used to cement bushings to blank and reel seat, cork to blank, and butt caps and other trim to cork and blank. Since over the life of a rod a great deal of pressure is placed on these parts, a strong, waterproof bond is required. There are many formulations of cold-setting, solvent-type adhesives available. Some that I have found to be quite good are Gudebrod Liquid Rod Cement, 3M Rubber Cement, and Pliobond. Pliobond, made by Goodyear, provides a strong flexible bond of all materials used in rod making. Its only draw-back is that it takes about three days to fully cure. One of the strongest bonds, but not quite as flexible, is obtained by using the two-solution epoxy glues, which cure by catalytic action.

Color preserver is a clear penetrating sealer. It is applied to the thread guide wrappings in order to preserve their color and avoid blotches when the protective varnish, or finish, coating is applied. There are various formulations, generally clear and having the consistency of water. Silver lacquer is sometimes used, since some rod builders feel it shrinks the wrappings. This is not silver in color, but almost clear with a slight amber tint. When applied over white thread, it has a tendency to impart a slight color cast, but is excellent with other colors.

Rod varnish is used to provide a tough protective coating over the guide wrappings. Sometimes it is also used to coat the entire blank, particularly on surf or heavy-duty saltwater rods. Coating the blank on other rods is not necessary, and the action of a light rod is stiffened slightly if the entire blank is varnished. For years the standard was Rodspar Varnish, which still does an excellent job. Some of the newer polyurethane and plastic-resin base varnishes are even better. You can also coat wrappings with fiberglass resin, or with a two-solution, thin epoxy finish. Whichever is chosen, it should dry as nearly clear and colorless as possible.

From your experience with fishing rods, I am sure you are already familiar with many of the components that go together to make up a rod. You may be a little doubtful about what is below the surface, or you may not be familiar with the terms used. Depending upon your experience, you may or may not know what constitutes quality in a given part. For all of these reasons we should review each of the various bits and pieces that might be used in the construction of a rod. Proper understanding here will eliminate frustrating mistakes later.

ROD PARTS

FERRULES

There are two kinds of ferrules used in rod building.

Rod ferrules are used to provide a removable joint between sections of the rod for transporting and storage. They are either mounted at the factory, or self-installed by the custom-rod builder. The best are made of anodized aluminum alloy with a rubber O-ring on the male piece, a solid fiberglass plug, or a fiberglass sleeve. For a more detailed discussion, see the preceding chapter on selection of the blank.

Butt ferrules are for use on casting rods, some spin-cast rods, and some light boat or trolling rods. The ferrule is placed on the butt end of the blank so the rod disassembles at the junction of blank and handle. The ferrule consists of only one piece, a male section that fits into a corresponding female section built into the handle. There are a variety of styles. Some simply make a tight sliding fit the same as regular ferrules. Others are knurled to provide a better grip by a collet chuck in the handle. In addition, some, such as the Fenwick butt ferrule, have a notch for perfect alignment in a matching handle or any handle accepting a 3/8-inch-diameter ferrule. Butt ferrules are made of anodized aluminum alloy for light and medium rods, and plated brass for some heavier rods.

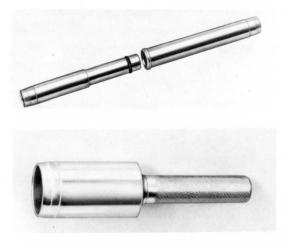

Anodized-aluminum ferrule with rubber O-ring.

Butt ferrule. This model has a knurled shank for a better grip.

Double-locking fly-reel
seat.

Sliding-hood fly-reel seat.

FIXED REEL SEAT

This component firmly holds the reel in place, preventing any movement or slippage. It consists of a tubular barrel which is threaded at one end. Attached to the opposite end of the barrel is a fixed hood into which slips one of the reel mounting feet. Another hood slides over the barrel to hold the other reel mounting foot. This sliding hood is securely locked into place with one or two knurled threaded rings. There are different types of fixed reel seats for the various rods.

Fly rods use a seat that is closed at one end with the hood or cup permanently primed to the barrel and forming the butt cap for the rod.

Spinning rods use a reel seat open at each end for location between the foregrip and the rear grip. The best reel seats for fly and spinning rods are made of lightweight anodized aluminum alloy and have two threaded locking rings.

Double-locking spinning-
reel seat.

31

Popping-rod reel seat.

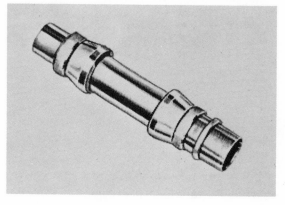

Big-game reel seat has
heavy machined hoods.

Trolling and boat rods use a reel seat similar to the above, but
with an additional piece—a matching male ferrule which fits into the
female ferrule (or barrel) of the reel seat. This separate male ferrule is
attached to the foregrip. Since trolling and boat rods need greater
strength and are often used in salt water, they are made of heavily
plated brass. Especially on these latter seats, but an advantage on all
seats, are the truncated or rounded threads. These are better than the
V-type, since they prevent sand or other grit from lodging in the
threads and provide greater wall strength. Reel seats are available in
various inside diameters to fit blanks of different sizes, and are installed over bushings or arbors.

REEL-SEAT BUSHINGS

Since the inside diameter of the reel seat is constant over its entire
length, yet must fit over a tapered blank of varying diameter, a bushing
or filler is needed. This bushing also forms a resilient pad between the

reel seat and the glass blank, protecting the important outer glass fibers from crushing. The inside diameter of the bushing must be shaped to fit the taper of the blank. It therefore is made of some easily worked material, such as wood, cork, or composition fiber. Generally, soft pine wood bushings are used on fly rods, cork on spinning rods, and wood or fiber on trolling and saltwater rods. However, any resilient material can be used to convert the taper to a constant diameter and to fill the space for a tight fit. Masking tape or medium-weight cotton string wound tightly around the blank and saturated with glue does very nicely.

NON-FIXED REEL SEATS

Spinning rod rings are used on light spinning rods and very light fly rods to keep weight to the very minimum. The one-piece rings encircle the cork grip and slide up over the reel feet to hold the reel in place. In addition to saving weight, they allow the reel to be positioned at various points to attain the balance most comfortable to the caster, and present more cork to the hand for a comfortable grip. Their principal disadvantage is that they do not hold the reel as securely as a fixed reel seat. They are made of metal, usually anodized aluminum, and often in various colors. There are a number of designs. Tapered rings merely rely on the even taper over the length of the ring to wedge themselves over the reel feet. Some tapered rings are knurled to help you tighten them into position. Swaged rings are swaged out (have a cup), which better enables them to fit any type of reel foot. Still another type are locking rings, which can also be moved to any position on the cork grip, but firmly lock over the reel foot by a threaded mechanism.

Rings for spinning reels: on left, swaged ring; on right, tapered ring.

Locking rings for spinning reels.

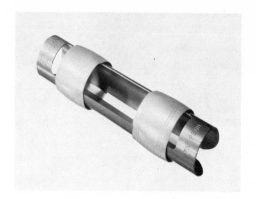

Sliding spinning-reel seat.

Sliding spinning reel seats consist of a thin, partially open barrel and swaged rings, which can be slid to any position on the cork grip. The swaged rings and the barrel then provide a compound squeezing action that grips both the reel feet and the cork grip. Such seats are quite light in weight and generally are made of anodized aluminum alloy. They will not hold a reel as securely as a fixed reel seat, but represent a compromise to the ultralight spinning rings.

GRIPS

Preassembled grips are most commonly made of specie cork rings, which have been preglued together and shaped (for discussion of grades of cork, see next paragraph). Grips are also made of composition cork, sometimes called burnt cork. This is ground cork which has been combined with thermoplastic bonding agents and cured in a mold. Some saltwater rod grips are made of rubber. A new type of resilient grip is made of Hypalon, a rubberlike plastic available in a variety of colors. All types come with a hole running the length of the grip, which you then shape to fit the taper of the blank. They are available in various lengths, diameters, and styles to fit different types and sizes of rods.

Cork rings, generally ½ inch thick, are used to form grips. They are glued to each other and to the rod blank, and then sanded to the desired shape. They are available in various outside and inside diameters. There are several grades of cork rings. "Specie cork" has the natural pits running lengthwise in the same direction as the center hole.

 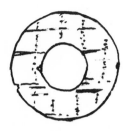

In specie cork (left), pits run the same direction as hole; in Mustad cork (right), pits run across the cork.

After sanding, the pits that appear are small. "Extra select grade specie cork" has less pits, but is scarce. "Mustad cork" is less desirable, since the pits run across the hole and often do not appear until after you have commenced sanding. As with specie cork, these are graded as to number and size of pits. "Handfilled cork" has the pits or holes filled with powdered cork, and is occasionally available in expensive preassembled custom grips.

Preformed grips and cork rings.

Straight casting-rod handle.

Adjustable-angle casting-rod handle.

Two-handed casting-rod handle.

Pistol-grip casting-rod handle.

HANDLES, BUTTS, AND HOSELS

Completed handle assemblies are used in the construction of some types of rods. Casting and spin-casting rods generally are taken apart at the junction of handle and blank. The preassembled handle has a female ferrule built into it, or a collet chuck to grip the male ferrule on the butt end of the blank. The handle has a built-in reel seat with locking screw and clamp. There is a "trigger" or hook for the index finger. The foregrip is extremely short and the hand grip may be either straight, set at a slight angle, or shaped like a pistol grip. Boat and trolling rods are most often made with a preassembled handle which includes an appropriate fixed reel seat and a separate companion male ferrule for attaching to the foregrip. The handles are 16 to 30 inches long and made of wood (hickory or ash). Some modern big-game trolling-rod handles, such as the Fenwick line, are made of fiberglass. The butt end may be fitted with a rubber butt cap or, in the case of big-game rods, with a gimbal (ball or knock) to keep the rod from turning in the rod holder.

Adjustable chuck handles are also made to fit spinning and fly rods. They are seldom used on custom or quality rods, and are more of a novelty for use in temporarily converting the tip sections of other rods to short, ultralight-action rods.

Detachable fighting butts are removable extensions, 4 to 6 inches long, used primarily on saltwater fly rods for fighting large fish.

Butt caps are used at the extreme end of the butt to protect the grip. On fly rods they are an integral part of the fixed reel seat. Butt caps are often made of plastic or rubber—the latter is best since it is more resilient, absorbs shocks, and provides a nonslip surface. They can easily be improvised from the caps sold in hardware stores to

More casting-rod handles.   Gimbals for big-game trolling rods.

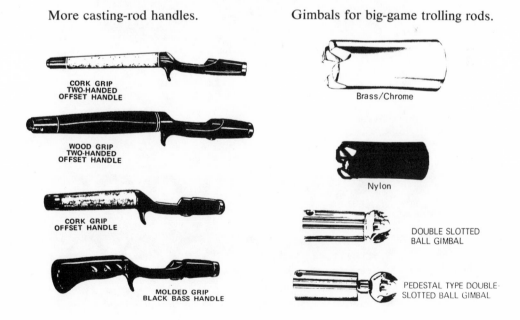

CORK GRIP
TWO-HANDED
OFFSET HANDLE

WOOD GRIP
TWO-HANDED
OFFSET HANDLE

CORK GRIP
OFFSET HANDLE

MOLDED GRIP
BLACK BASS HANDLE

Brass/Chrome

Nylon

DOUBLE SLOTTED
BALL GIMBAL

PEDESTAL TYPE DOUBLE-
SLOTTED BALL GIMBAL

cover the bottoms of tubular metal table legs, or made from wood or plastic. On some saltwater rods they are larger and often shaped like a ball or mushroom cap.

Winding checks are flat rings used to provide a finishing piece at the end of the grip where the blank emerges. They are made of anodized aluminum or plated brass and are available in a wide range of sizes to fit the diameter of the blank. A rubber washer can also be used effectively.

Butt caps. The two plastic caps on the left are made for the purpose and are commercially available. The two on the right are protective caps made to fit over the legs of tubular metal furniture. The one on the end is rubber, and the other is plastic. They can be cut to any length and make excellent heavy-duty butt caps.

Metal winding checks.

Rod hosels are sometimes used as a finishing piece at either or both ends of the grip to provide a taper from the diameter of the grip to the diameter of the blank. Generally made of plastic or rubber, about ¾ inch to 1½ inches long, they are available in a number of colors. Besides those that you can purchase, you can make your own of wood or any other easily worked material. A hosel offers some protection to the end of the grip, but it is principally decorative.

ROD WRAPPING THREAD

Thread is used to secure the guides to the blank and for trim and finishing in front of grip, at ferrules, and at tip-top. Both silk and nylon are used. Silk doesn't stretch and has brighter colors, but will rot eventually if not adequately protected. Nylon is stronger, won't rot, and is less expensive. However, it has the disadvantage of stretching, and in time the wrapping may come loose. Sizes from very fine to heavy are used. The finer thread makes a neater wrap, but is not as strong. Some general suggestions on size: sizes O and OO in silk or nylon for ultralight spinning and light fly rods; size A for normal fly rods and spinning; size C+, D, or E for heavier rods such as heavy saltwater rods and surf rods. Wrapping thread is available in solid colors; two-tone, which gives a tiny zigzag or tweedy effect; and varigated (space dyed), with color changing every so many inches to provide alternating bands of color.

Rod wrapping thread. From left to right: solid-color; variegated; two-color space-dyed; multi-color space-dyed ("rainbow").

GUIDES

Guides are ringlike devices made of metal and wire which are placed along the length of the blank to guide the line from reel to tip-top. Frequently just about the only difference between a cheap, poor-quality rod and one of top quality is the guides and the windings. The blank used may even be the same. In commercially made, mass-produced rods, the most costly item is labor—and guides must be hand-wrapped onto the rod. Second only to labor in cost is the hardware. Unfortunately, most fishermen cannot tell the difference between good and inferior guides. In fact, I know of one wholesale dealer who mentions this very fact in his catalog and suggests the use of less expensive guides as a way of keeping costs down and profits high. In purchasing a rod, many fishermen do not take the time to inspect the windings, or know what to look for. Sometimes in the rush of mass production, the guides are not spaced correctly or are not mounted on the correct side of the blank. Another problem is that there may be too few guides and they may not be the correct size.

Since in an average day of casting and fishing an incredible amount of line will pass through the guides (as much as 10 or 12 miles), they should be of the hardest, most wear-resistant materials available. Fine-diameter monofilament lines pick up microscopic grains of dirt and sand, wearing grooves into the guides. In time these grooves become sharp enough to fray and weaken the line.

The hardest materials are tungsten carbide, agate, and the new aluminum oxide. Agate is a semi-precious stone which is diamond-ground and polished. Its greatest drawbacks are that it is relatively heavy and cracks easily from a sharp blow. As a result, it has largely been replaced by tungsten carbide. Guides made from tungsten carbide are generally sold under the name Carboloy, which is a registered trade name of the General Electric Company. For years it has been known as the hardest man-made material and will scratch the natural sapphire. It is impervious to the corrosive action of salt water. The newest material on the fishing scene is an aluminum oxide compound. This is a ceramic material developed for missile and spacecraft nose-cones. It is reportedly harder than the time-proven tungsten carbide, and when diamond-ground and polished presents considerably less

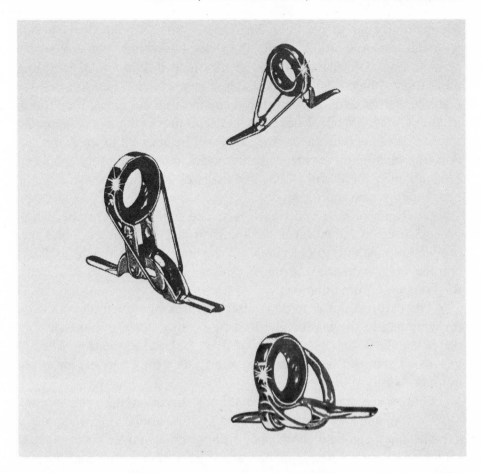

Aluminum-oxide guides. The center model can be folded against the rod when not in use.

Construction of aluminum-oxide guides. The inner hard ring fits into a cushioning plastic ring, which fits into the stainless-steel outer band. The frame is one-piece construction.

41

friction and wear to the line. The "speed" line of guides first offered with this material utilize a plastic shock-absorbing ring around the ceramic ring. The plastic ring is in turn held in place in a light, one-piece (no welding or soldering) stainless-steel frame. The same ceramic material is to be available shortly in another line of guides, the "Sintox Missile Guide." While I have not yet seen these guides, the manufacturer informs me that the ceramic ring will be epoxied to the frame and that the aluminum oxide will be even more smoothly polished. Undoubtedly, there will be further research and development of this new exciting material for guides.

Next in hardness and wear resistance is the hard chrome-plating process used in industrial applications to add long life to high-speed production machinery. On guides, it is generally referred to as "hard chrome" or "industrial chrome" plating, and is considerably better than regular chrome plating.

The hard ring of a guide is attached to a support frame with feet for wrapping to the blank. The best frames are made of hard-chrome-plated stainless-steel wire, which is silver-soldered to the ring. The less expensive stamped frames are not nearly as strong and the rings pop out more easily.

Guides are made in many styles for the different types of rods.

Casting and spin-cast guides consist of a circular ring mounted on a frame. They can be distinguished from spinning guides since they are set lower, closer to the blank, and are of heavier construction. A set of casting or spin-cast guides do not vary as much in ring size as do a set of spinning guides. The sizes usually range from about 7 millimeters to about 10 millimeters.

Wire-frame casting guides. From left to right: regular; braced; bridge type.

Spinning guides are also made of rings set on frames. The frames, however, are lighter and higher, holding the rings a greater distance away from the blank. This is necessary on spinning rods since the line flows from the stationary spool of the reel in large loops and must be prevented from slapping against the blank. For the same reason the guides toward the butt must be considerably larger to funnel the line along the blank toward the tip-top. The larger the spinning rod and the reel used with it, the larger must be the guides near the butt. On 6½-foot to 9-foot medium spin rods, the butt guide should at least be 26–35mm. Casting distance is often limited on commercially made rods because too small a butt guide has been used to hold down costs. Unnecessary friction is set up when the line is "choked" as it flows from the spool. The high-set, large-diameter guides near the butt on heavy-duty spinning rods (such as saltwater and surf rods) require a bracing. Such a guide has an additional reinforced wire arch for extra support. When using size 30mm and over, a braced guide is recommended on any spinning rod.

V-frame spinning-rod guide.

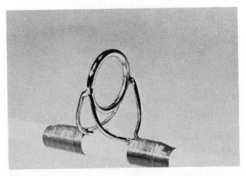

U-frame spinning-rod guide.

Braced-wire spinning-rod guide.

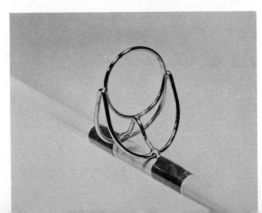

Foulproof guide.

Snake guides for fly rod.

Ultralight and light spinning guides. There is a guide made of entirely different design called "foulproof" that is particularly well suited to ultralight and light spinning rods. These are made of one piece of spring-tempered Monel wire with hard-chrome plating. The center of the wire is coiled to form the ring and each end becomes a mounting foot. There are no soldered joints and the design allows the guide to flex with the action of the rod. They are lighter than regular spinning guides and the gauge of the wire varies with the size of the guide. The original of this type is the Foulproof—a registered trade name of Gudebrod Brothers. While there are other guides of similar style, only the Foulproof is, to my knowledge, made of the more expensive Monel material.

Fly-rod guides. Fly rods usually have a butt guide (called the stripping guide) of the ring type. The size is about 8–10mm and is identical to a casting-rod guide. Traditionally, all other fly-rod guides are one-piece hardened wire in the form of a spiral, called snake guides. They are small, light, and hold the line close to the blank. They are graduated in size, smaller toward the tip-top. The better ones are made of stainless steel or tungsten steel, and some are finished in black nickel to eliminate flash, which may scare wary trout. More recently, the larger saltwater fly rods (and some bass-bugging rods) have been equipped with the "foulproof" guides used for ultralight spinning rods.

It is claimed that these resist abrasion better, prolonging fly-line life, and that the line shoots through the "foulproof" guide 50 percent easier than through snake guides. From personal experience, I definitely feel the line shoots more easily, permitting greater distance. The line is not held as close to the blank as with snake guides, nor are as many guides needed. Friction is therefore reduced.

Trolling and big-game rod guides. For the freshwater and light saltwater trolling and boat rods, the same guides as on casting rods are used. About the only difference is that they are a little heavier and more sturdy. When it comes to handling the tremendous strength and speed of ocean-dwelling big-game fish, the grooved-roller guide is needed. The roller support frames are high and exceptionally strong. Friction must be reduced to the absolute minimum. Some guide rollers are mounted on impregnated Oilite bearings and others on sealed ball bearings. The tip-top on this type of rod is also fitted with a similar roller.

Braced saltwater guides. The three on the left (A, B, C) have Carboloy rings; the three on the right (a, b, c) have stainless steel rings.

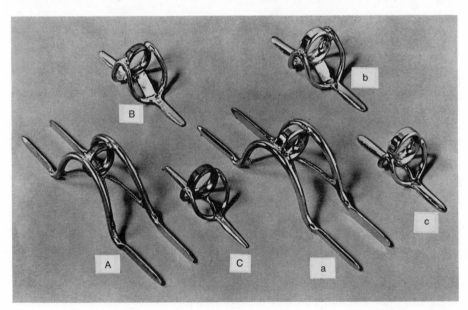

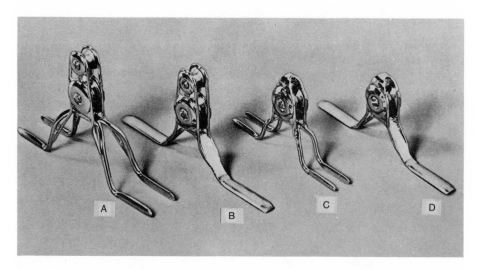

Roller guides. A, double guide, straddle mount; B, double guide, top mount; C, single guide, straddle mount; D, single guide, top mount.

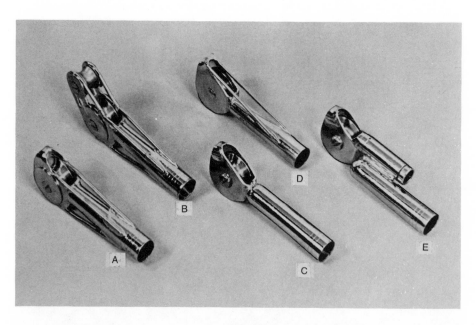

Roller tops. A, single; B, double; C, single with stamped frame; D, single with stamped frame, riveted; E, single, swivel-action.

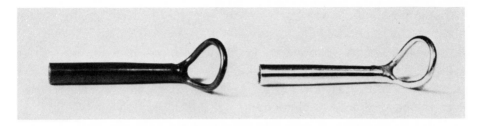

Fly-rod tip-tops, in black nickel and chrome.

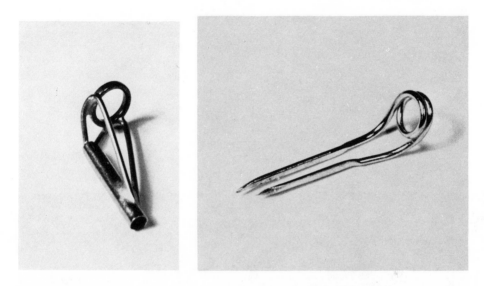

Wire-frame tip-top.   Foulproof tip-top.

Tip-tops. Of all the guides on a rod, the tip-top receives the most wear, and should be of the hardest material. Tungsten-carbide (Carboloy) tip-tops are the best for casting, spin-casting, spinning, and light trolling rods. Fly-rod tip-tops are traditionally pear-shaped and formed by a loop of hardened wire inserted into a tapered tube. The wire is silver-soldered and the whole assembly heavily plated (some with a black nickel finish). Some rod builders use tungsten-carbide tip-tops on heavy-duty fly rods, especially saltwater fly rods. Others feel the tungsten carbide is too abrasive to modern fly lines. Personally, I have used these tops on my saltwater rods, and, while the lines have shown evidence of wear, I do not attribute it solely to the tungsten carbide.

Perhaps the solution will be found in tip-tops of the new aluminum-oxide ceramic material. Tip-tops of all styles are available in sizes to fit the tip of the blank. The size is given in 64ths of an inch and represents the inside diameter of the tube.

Hookkeeper. Last but not least, one of the smallest, least expensive, yet most practical components — the little hookkeeper. This is a U-shaped piece of wire with flattened feet for wrapping to the blank just above the foregrip. It provides a convenient, safe place to temporarily store the fly or lure when the rod is strung with line. It eliminates the destructive habit of sticking the hook into the foregrip. Always include it.

The complete components for a spinning rod.

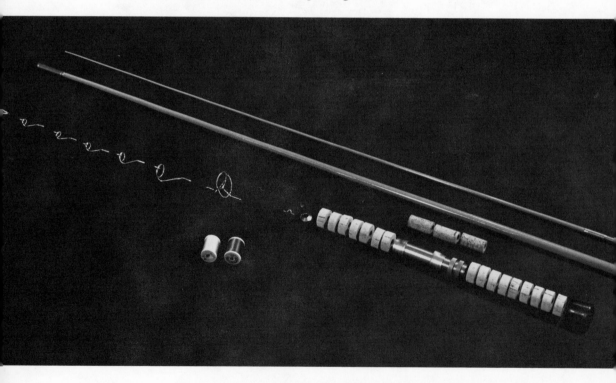

SIZE OF GUIDES

In our discussion of guides, I made some reference to the proper sizes for some types of rods. However, you are still faced with the problem of how many guides you should place on a certain rod and the proper size of each. The number of guides on a rod determines the number of stress points and the amount of pressure at each point. The stress point is located midway between any two guides. The farther apart the guides are, the greater the pressure on the point between. If the number of guides is increased, the stress is distributed over more points and is thus reduced. However, if too many guides are placed on a rod, they will add too much weight, change the action of the rod, and increase friction against the line in casting. It is, therefore, important to determine the correct number of guides for the rod you are building, as well as the size of each guide. Catalogs usually list sets of matched guides that appear to present a savings over purchasing individual guides. The number of guides is given, but the sizes are frequently omitted. In spinning guides in particular, the sizes in these sets may be too small for the butt guide and other large-diameter guides. Unless the sizes are given and they match the sizes you want, you will do better to purchase the guides individually.

From our discussion about the problems of commercially made rods, I would caution you not to fall back on the number and size you find on these rods. The manufacturers' approaches to the number of guides run the gamut from skimpy to overdoing it. In spinning rods in particular, too small a butt guide and adjacent guide are often used to keep costs down and make the rod appear more streamlined to the unknowing fisherman. It is amazing how casting distance can be increased with the proper large-size gathering or butt guides on a spinning rod, and the proper guide spacing for that particular blank.

The lists that follow should help you in determining both number and size of guides for various rods. They represent a great deal of experience and experimentation on the part of quite a few people, but they are not to be considered absolute. They are a starting point to help you in designing your custom rod.

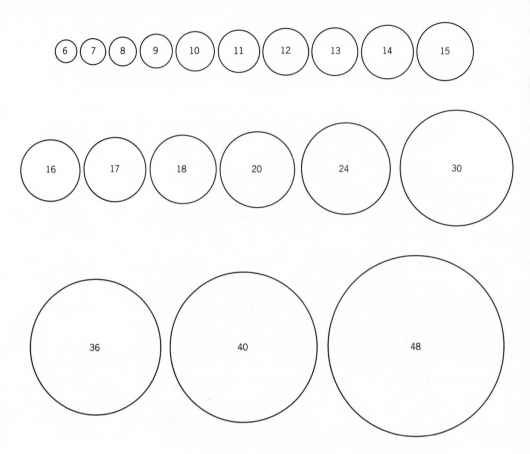

Millimeter scale for guides.

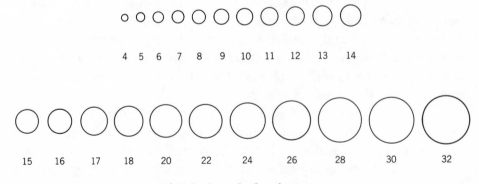

4 5 6 7 8 9 10 11 12 13 14

15 16 17 18 20 22 24 26 28 30 32

1/64-inch scale for tip-tops.

7'–8½' fly rod

Butt guide	8mm casting guide
Snake guides (6–8)	Stainless steel, graduated in size
Tip	Hard-chrome pear-shape or light Carboloy casting tip-top

9' fly rod (Alternate #1)

Butt guide	10mm casting guide
Second guide	8mm casting guide
Snake guides (8)	Stainless steel, graduated in size
Tip	Hard-chrome pear-shape or light Carboloy casting tip-top

9' fly rod (Alternate #2)

Butt guide	10–12mm casting guide
Foulproof (2)	$3/8''$
Foulproof (3)	$5/16''$
Foulproof (3)	$7/32''$
Tip	Foulproof or light Carboloy tip-top

5'–6' ultralight spinning rod

Foulproof	$7/8''-1''$
Foulproof	$5/8''$
Foulproof	$5/16''$
Foulproof	$7/32''$
Tip	Light Carboloy or Foulproof tip-top

6'–7' spinning rod (alternate #1)

Foulproof	$1\,1/8''-1\,1/4''$
Foulproof	$3/4''-5/8''$
Foulproof	$1/2''$
Foulproof	$3/8''$
Foulproof	$5/16''$
Foulproof	$1/4''$
Tip	Carboloy spinning tip-top

6'–7' spinning rod (Alternate #2)

Butt guide	30mm braced spinning
#5	26mm high spinning
#4	16mm high spinning
#3	14mm high spinning
#2	10mm high spinning
#1	8mm high spinning
Tip	Carboloy spinning tip-top

7'–9' spinning rod

Butt guide	35–40mm braced spinning
#5	30mm braced or 28mm high spinning
#4	16mm high spinning
#3	14mm high spinning
#2	10mm high spinning
#1	8mm high spinning
Tip	Carboloy spinning tip-top

5½'–6½' casting or spin-cast rod

Butt guide	12mm casting
#4, #5	10mm casting
#1, #2, #3	8mm casting
Tip	Carboloy casting tip-top

7'–8½' casting or spin-cast rod

Butt guide	14mm casting (preferably braced)
#5	12mm casting
#3, #4	10mm casting
#1, #2	8mm casting
Tip	Carboloy casting tip-top

Trolling rods (length of blank normally 5¼'–5⅓')
(Note: This type of rod varies in its diameter and strength.)

Butt guide	1 13/16" high (roller guide)
#4	1 5/8" high (roller guide)
#3	1 1/2" high (roller guide)
#2	1 3/8" high (roller guide)
#1	1 1/4" high (roller guide)
Tip	Roller tip-top

4. Designing Your Rod

By now you have a rough idea of how a rod is put together and a fairly comprehensive understanding of each of the parts that may be used. Next comes the creative part—designing your rod. Chances are that you will find this to be one of the most exciting aspects of rod building. Here is where your personality is injected into the finished product. Your objective is to design the best possible tool for the specific fishing you have in mind. You will create a rod that in appearance, style, and color is everything you always wanted.

Your starting point is the selection of the blank, and all the variables we discussed earlier will have to be considered. From there you evaluate all of the parts that will be used, and in the process you design your rod. The ideas presented in this chapter are to assist you in the design. Actual instruction on how to do these things will, where needed, be covered later in Chapter 6.

MODIFYING THE ACTION

As was discussed in Chapter 2 on selection of the blank, the action of a rod is described in terms of speed: the speed with which the recoil occurs and, therefore, the speed necessary in the timing of our casting. As I am sure you realize by this time, I am partial to the more moderate-action rods whether it be for fly, spinning, or casting. Since blanks designed with this type of action are not yet as numerous as I would like, I have frequently modified the action to slow it down a bit. You, no doubt, have your own preference in this category. You may find two blanks both designed to handle the proper weight, etc., but one is a little too fast and the other a little too slow. In that case, you may want to select the faster-action model and then take steps in construction to slow it down somewhat. Whatever your tastes, the objective is to obtain exactly the action you desire. Here are some techniques for modifying rod action that have worked well for me.

One thing you can do is place the ferrule closer toward the butt, giving you a longer tip section. This moves the flat spot from the joint farther along the blank before it meets the resistance of the ferrule.

Another technique is to order a blank longer than you want and then cut off a section from the butt. You now have a blank with a greater percentage of bend, or a slower action. This works well when you are purchasing a blank that has the ferrules factory-installed at the midpoint. By shortening the butt you move the ferrule lower on the rod. You obtain rod action and feel as described in the preceding paragraph, but have dispensed with the job of installing the ferrule yourself.

If you don't want the ferrule in the middle of the blank, you can install it closer to the butt, or you can buy a longer blank, mid-ferruled at the factory, and cut down the butt section.

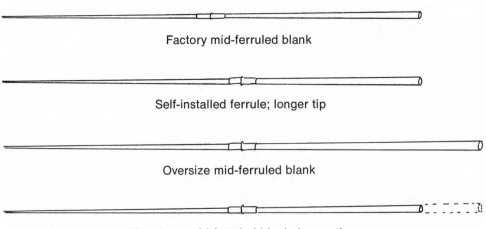

Factory mid-ferruled blank

Self-installed ferrule; longer tip

Oversize mid-ferruled blank

Cut-down mid-ferruled blank; longer tip

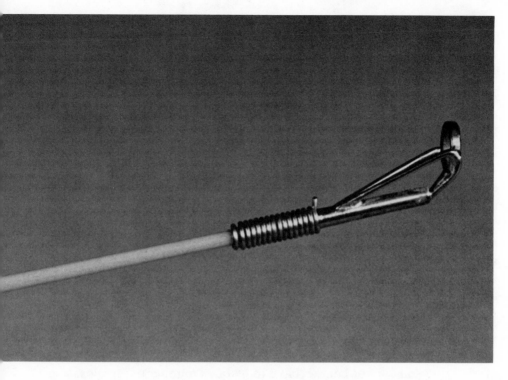

Soft lead wire wrapped around rod tip for testing action.

More weight concentrated at or near the tip of a rod will cause it to bend a little farther on the cast and slow the rate of recoil. If this is your objective, use a heavier tip-top. You can also add more guides closer to the tip, and they can be of a heavier type. A good method to determine the amount of weight needed is to assemble the rod, but only tape the guides in place, and go outside and cast with it. Wrap the tip with varying amounts of soft lead wire such as used by flytiers to weight their flys. This wire is available in .020 and .040 diameters and, incidentally, has many different fishing applications. For example, it can be used for adding a small amount of "twist-on" weight at or near your fly, lure, or bait. Another use when fishing is to temporarily slow the action of a rod to enable you to cast lighter lures than that for which the rod was generally designed. Just wrap the tip with some of the soft wire. I always keep a small coil in my tackle box.

I once built a bass-bugging fly rod that was great in every respect except that its action was too fast for me. After testing by casting with increasing amounts of soft lead wire, I finally found my answer. It was certainly unorthodox, but it worked perfectly. What I did was to use a large Carboloy spinning tip-top with a barrel having a larger inside diameter tube than the size of my rod tip. I first wrapped the tip with fine lead wire and cemented it in place. After it dried, I then cemented the oversize spinning tip-top over the lead wire. A careful job of building up wrapping thread next to the tip-top resulted in a natural appearance, and the combined weight of the lead and larger tip-top slowed the rod action to just what I wanted.

If you are building an ultralight or light spinning rod from a slow-action or moderate-action blank, and want to preserve that action, consider using foulproof guides, which flex with the rod and are very light in weight. Personally, I am not too fond of the foulproof tip-tops and suggest that in this case you use the lightest Carboloy one you can find. But if you feel the heavier Carboloy slows the action more than you want, then by all means use the very light foulproof tip-top.

When building a "pack rod" that has to break down into a number of sections, you will, of course, have to install a number of ferrules. It is always hard to preserve good smooth action in this type of rod (including one that has glass-to-glass ferrules). Therefore, keep to a slow- or moderate-action blank right from the start. Otherwise, the additional flat spots will cause the rod to cast somewhat like a broomstick. If the rod is a light rod of up to about 7 feet or 7½ feet maximum, you will preserve action better and keep weight down by using the shorter "mini-ferrules" or "micro-ferrules." To further offset the added weight of the extra ferrules it helps to use the lightweight foulproof guides.

KINDS OF GUIDES

This subject has already been covered rather extensively, but in designing your rod you should now decide on the guides you will use. If building a spinning rod, consider the previously suggested braced guide for the butt guide if it is 30mm or over. On saltwater spinning rods (particularly surf rods) and long, heavy-duty freshwater rods, it is a good idea to use braced guides for all the larger guides at the butt end of the rod. The added strength of this type of guide is needed for protection when the rod is in transit, either in a roof rack of a car or in a travel case. Rods often receive quite a beating in a boat, and the large butt guides of a spinning rod are the most vulnerable.

On fly rods you have the choice of snake guides in bright or black finish, and foulproof guides. If you are going to cast a forward-taper line long distances, you will find the foulproof guides enable you to get a better "shoot" of the line.

The guides you use on a boat or trolling rod are definitely a function of the kind of fishing. Freshwater and light saltwater rods can be assembled with regular—but heavy-duty—casting-rod guides. As the size and strength of the quarry you are seeking increases, you need to move up to a roller tip, and finally to roller guides for large saltwater game fish.

HANDLE ASSEMBLY

From the standpoint of appearance, the entire handle assembly presents the greatest opportunity for creative personal design. If you want a rod that is immediately recognizable as custom-built, this is the section on which to concentrate. Your choice of materials, style, and trim can result in something that is truly distinctive. I do not mean to overlook the functional aspects of custom design. They are paramount. But, if you want to get fancy, here is one place you can do it.

Reel seat

The heart of the handle section of a rod is the reel seat. Your choice of the type of reel seat will be dictated by such factors as the weight of the rod, the kinds of fish you intend to catch, and your preference for the material in touch with your hand as you grip the rod. On an extremely light fly rod or an ultralight spinning rod, select sliding metal rings over cork for your design. This keeps hardware to a minimum and preserves the delicate, wisplike feel of these rods. A light freshwater spinning rod might be just right with a sliding reel seat. However, on a similar light bonefish rod you will need to have the reel anchored as securely as possible, which requires a double-locking reel seat of anodized aluminum. Cold-weather fishing is more comfortable when your hand is on cork rather than on cold metal, so you will be happier if you use sliding rings—perhaps the locking type if you are seeking larger fish, or the customized seat with cork insert discussed next.

If you are adventuresome and want something unique, customize a fixed reel seat. To do this, cut out the center section of the barrel between the threads and the fixed hood. This is done quite easily on aluminum with a fine-tooth saw. When mounting the seat on the blank, replace the removed metal section with an appropriate length and diameter of either hardwood or cork rings. The choice of wood or cork depends on your preferences for feel and appearance.

If the rod you are designing is a heavy model for saltwater fishing, you will find a heavily plated brass reel seat stronger than one of anodized aluminum. Both will resist the corrosive action of salt water, but here strength is most important.

Standard reel seat (rear) has been customized by removing center barrel and replacing it with wood insert.

This custom fixed reel seat for a very light spinning rod has insert of burnt-cork and specie-cork rings. The tapered foregrip is wrapped with thread and epoxy-finished. The rear grip is specie cork, with one burnt-cork ring and a butt plate at the end.

GRIPS AND HANDLES

Built around the reel seat are the grips or handle. On a fly rod you have a choice of quite a few standard shapes developed over the years, or you can create your own. Cork is easily shaped with sandpaper, so the diameter can easily be sized to the grip of your hand. Similarly, a depression for your thumb can be crafted if you like. Your preference for balance and where you like to grip the rod will dictate the length of your design. Such custom grips are best constructed of cork rings, but it is also possible to plan on modifying the shape of preassembled grips.

Fly-rod grip shapes.

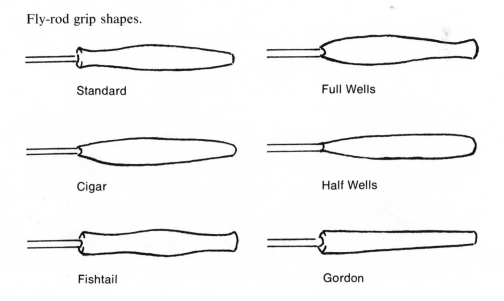

Standard

Full Wells

Cigar

Half Wells

Fishtail

Gordon

Ritz

Fly-rod grip shapes (cont.)

European

Heavy-duty saltwater, with fighting foregrip

Customizing ideas for "standard" fly-rod grips.

Standard cork grip

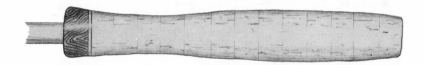

Wood hosel with thin, light-colored plastic ring

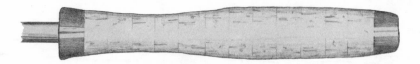

Plastic hosels at either end

Burnt-cork rings

Customizing ideas for "cigar" fly-rod grips.

Cigar grip with three burnt-cork rings

Plastic hosel

Wood hosels faced with light-colored plastic

Plastic hosel on front, wood-and-plastic hosel on rear

Handle assembly for very light fly rod. The reel seat is all cork and utilized two sliding metal rings.

Detachable fighting butt for heavy-duty fly rod.

If you are designing a fly rod for salt water or salmon, you may want to consider a detachable fighting butt. One of the problems encountered in taking large heavy fish on a fly is that the reel seat is at the very bottom of the rod. This makes it difficult to brace the rod against you and turn the reel comfortably at the same time. The detachable fighting butt, carried easily in your pocket until you have a fish on, is a simple solution. It is better than building the rod with a permanent fighting butt affixed below the reel, since this interferes with casting and shifts the balance of the rod. You will need a special fly-reel seat that is not closed on the bottom. Instead, it has a built-in socket (female ferrule) which accepts the male ferrule of the detachable butt. The seat and completed butt are sold in matched sets. You can also fashion your own detachable butt by using a matching set consisting of special reel seat and male ferrule.

In designing a spinning-rod handle that is to use sliding rings, or a sliding reel seat, you will plan only one long cork grip or handle that is flared at each end. Or, you could flare only the forward part of the handle and use a larger, slip-over butt cap to prevent the rings from sliding off that end.

A spinning rod with a fixed reel seat calls for a design made up of a foregrip and a rear grip or handle. The length of the rear grip depends upon whether you intend to use one or two hands to cast the rod, and the amount of leverage you need to apply. Medium saltwater and surf rods have quite long rear grips. Design the length to fit your build and casting style for the type of fishing intended.

In this type of handle you can design one long section of uninterrupted cork, or you can split the rear grip into two separate parts with the bare blank between. The exposed section of blank may be covered with wrapping thread according to your tastes. The split sections of the rear grip can be made of cork or preformed composition-rubber grips fashioned for this purpose.

On the fixed-reel-seat spinning rod, determine the location of the reel seat for the balance and feel that is most comfortable to you. Great freedom is yours in the design of fore and rear grips. Apply the same concepts as discussed under fly-rod grips.

Plan also on the finishing parts of your handle assembly. The forward end of the grip where the blank emerges can be trimmed with a commercially available metal winding check. A similar winding check can be fashioned from plastic or from a rubber washer of the correct size. The taper of a foregrip can be designed so that it is continued by a rod hosel to a smooth transition to the diameter of the blank. You can create an even longer piece of trim by combining a matching butt cap (with the bottom removed) with a rod hosel. The resulting compound taper can be quite attractive. Rod hosels of your own design can be shaped from wood.

Two styles of two-handed spinning rods.

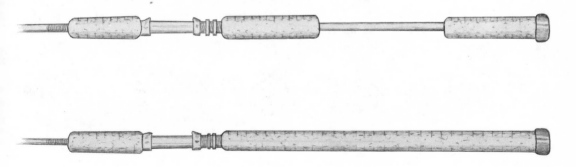

The other end of your handle assembly will contain some sort of butt cap to protect the cork and enhance the beauty. The butt cap can continue the taper, or straight lines, of the rear grip and be mounted so that the outside diameter of the cap is the same as the cork where the two meet. Or the butt cap can simply be slipped over the end of the cork grip. Another approach is a flat disk of metal or plastic which is glued or screwed into place and forms a butt plate. This end of the handle can be treated the same as the forward end with a matching hosel.

One way to customize a spinning or fly handle is to include one or more wood or colored-plastic rings in place of cork rings. Walnut and cherry, being dark, really set off the cork grip. Their finished appearance is greatly improved by bracketing each wood ring with a thin ring of white or colored plastic. The size is a matter of your own taste. I have found ½- or ¼-inch-thick wood bracketed by ⅛-inch-thick plastic to be very attractive. Important to the design of such trim is to make sure that the rings will not be placed under your hand when you grip the rod in the normal fashion. If you decide to use insert rings, try to carry through the color scheme in your guide wrappings. This really makes a beautiful rod. For example, if you are going to use walnut or cherry wood rings bracketed with thin rings of white plastic in the handle assembly, then use dark-brown thread for wrapping the guides with a narrow trim wrap of white thread. Similarly, walnut or cherry

Rubber butt plates can be made from devices readily available at hardware stores. The one on the far left is a rubber "foot" with screw. The others are washers of various types.

A custom spinning-rod handle. Wood trim ring faced with plastic for foregrip; wood insert in reel seat; wood hosel faced with plastic; rubber butt plate.

with thin yellow plastic can be matched on the rod with brown wraps trimmed in yellow. If you make your insert rings of colored plastic instead of wood, even more color combinations are possible. Utilize whatever color combinations please you. Just remember that good design consists of the development of one theme throughout. The handle assembly is a great place to be creative if you are so inclined. For stimulation and ideas, check the rods at your sporting goods dealer or the pictures in catalogs—then develop *your* theme for *your* custom rod.

Casting and spin-cast rods. Admittedly there is less room for custom designing in building a casting or spin-cast rod, since the blank is plugged into an already manufactured handle. You will, however, have to decide on the style and make of handle for your rod. On a long rod you may need to include a rod ferrule in addition to the butt ferrule. In some cases you may want to modify the grip on the manufactured handle. You can strip the cork away and build your own handle of different length or shape, and possibly include wood trim rings.

Standard casting-rod handle has custom grip of alternating burnt cork and specie cork. Thin white plastic ring separates butt cap and cork.

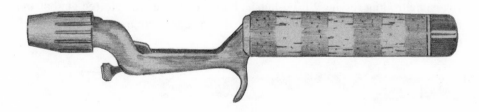

"Boots" Voigt makes a beautiful handle for his custom casting rods by modifying the sleek new speed handles made by Fuji. These handles have a rather long rear cork grip with a thin taper. "Boots" removes the cork from the ½-inch-diameter glass tube running the length of the grip. He cuts this shorter and builds a new thicker and shorter cork grip, which terminates in a rubber butt cap. In similar fashion you can create your own custom casting-rod handles.

Boat or trolling rods. You can, of course, use a completed handle-and-reel-seat assembly. This can be installed just as it is, or it can be modified. You can also purchase the components and build it yourself. The do-it-yourself approach will enable you to end up with exactly what you want and to have a more custom appearance. Here are some ideas for modifying, or building from parts, that you may want to consider. A cork foregrip can be shaped to a taper that goes all the way

Custom foregrip. Cork is tapered to diameter of blank, then protected and decorated with thread wrap.

Big-game trolling rod has "fired-finish" hickory handle with slotted gimbal and machined-hood locking reel seat. Each end of cork foregrip has wood hosel, one side faced with thin white plastic.

66

down to the diameter of the blank where it emerges from the grip. The forward portion of this cork taper can then be protected with a thread wrap which continues down over the cork and up a portion of the blank. This wrap can be fairly plain or can be quite fancy with contrasting-color overwrapped trim. This makes for a unique eye-catching design. The wood handle can be finished in various ways. It can be left clear and varnished, or it can be stained any color you desire with thinned paint. Using a torch, you can lightly burn the surface of the wood, then rub with fine steel wool for a unique "fired" finish. I saw an unusual set of custom boat rods in which the wood had been darkened with a torch in random spots for a "leopard" finish. If you are talented and have access to a lathe, you may even want to turn your own handle. If you do, use quality, straight-grained hickory which has been air dried. Whatever route you take, the length of the wood handle is an important consideration. It should fit you and the fishing you will do with the rod.

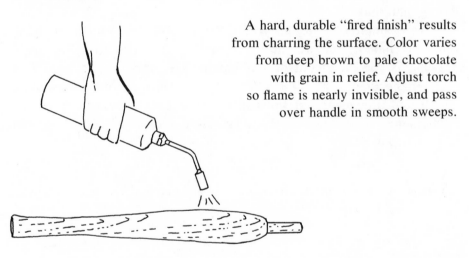

A hard, durable "fired finish" results from charring the surface. Color varies from deep brown to pale chocolate with grain in relief. Adjust torch so flame is nearly invisible, and pass over handle in smooth sweeps.

Brush charred surface with a soft wire brush or stiff scrub brush. Stroke lightly with the grain to rake out soft char until desired shade is reached. Seal the surface with paste wax. Repeated waxing builds a whitish fleck that enhances the finish.

These are the items you will be considering when you design your rod. Don't make the mistake of trusting your memory with all of it. Use the same approach any designer uses—make a sketch. It need not be elaborate, and you have no need for artistic ability. Some simple pencil lines on a sheet of tablet paper will do nicely. The important thing is that you can interpret your rendering.

Actually, I make two sketches. The simplest consists essentially of a line that represents the entire length of the rod. I do not bother to work out locations of guides or mark them on the sketch. I do mark the tip size, location and size of ferrules, and a very rough outline of the handle. The second sketch is just of the handle section of the rod and includes a breakdown of all the parts I intend to use. There is no need to draw it to scale; "eyeball" approximations are fine. Make it large enough so the components are easily recognizable and there is room to carefully label each part. The labeling will make the drawings easier for you to follow and will provide an invaluable checklist for ordering materials.

An example of a design sketch for a 7-foot one-handed spinning rod is included. The top line represents the entire rod. The main drawing is for the detail of the handle assembly. On it were first marked the diameter of the blank at the primary points. Next, the length and dimensions of the main components were added. In the next chapter we will use the same sketch to add the individual components needed.

A typical design sketch, showing whole rod and detail of handle.

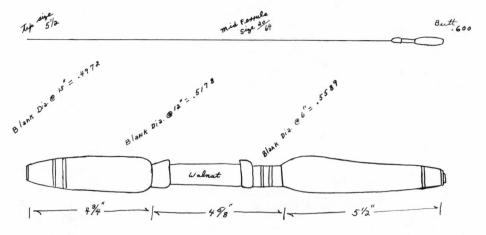

5. Ordering Materials

The biggest problem we all face in ordering the parts for our rod is getting the correct sizes so that everything fits together. After anxiously awaiting delivery, it is terribly frustrating to find that we cannot proceed because we have the wrong size part. This can be easily avoided if you will do a little simple arithmetic and think through the sizing of each component. Your sketch is the place to work this out, and it should have the sizes marked directly on it.

The first bit of math you need to do is to work out the approximate diameter of the blank at all key points. These points would be: the location of ferrules if you are going to install them yourself, the tip size, and in the case of a casting rod, the butt size (for a butt ferrule). If you are building a spinning or fly rod, work out the diameters of the blank at key intervals over that section of rod which will contain the handle and grip assembly: the butt, forward end of rear grip, each end of reel seat, ends of foregrip, and location of winding check or rod hosel.

Let's see how this works. Among the information listed in the catalog for a particular spinning-rod blank might appear the following:

Length	Butt size (inches)	Mid size (64ths)	Tip size (64ths)
7'	.600	20	5 1/2

On my first sketch would be marked "tip size 5½" and, assuming I was going to install the ferrule at the midpoint, "ferrule size 20/64."

To determine the approximate blank diameters on the butt end, where the handle assembly is to be built, first convert the mid size of 20/64 to inches (consult the Conversion Table at the end of this chapter). You will find that 20/64 = .3125 inch. Half the blank length is 3½ feet or 42 inches, so you know that over that length the blank tapers from .600 inch (butt) to .3125 inch (midsize). Subtracting .3125 from .600, you find the amount of the taper is .2875 inch.

Assuming you are building a one-handed spinning rod, you need to get an approximation of blank diameters over about the first 15 inches from the butt end. Indications at 6-inch intervals will be sufficient. The bottom half of the blank is 3½ feet or 42 inches long, and contains seven 6-inch intervals. Therefore, divide .2875 (the amount of the taper) by 7 (the number of 6-inch intervals) and you will find the dimensional drop from the butt will be about .04107 inch for each 6-inch interval as you progress toward the midpoint.

To review:

```
  .6000  (butt size)
−.3125  (mid size)
  .2875  (amount of taper)
```

```
Length of blank section: 3 ½ feet = 42 inches
42 ÷ 6 = 7 (number of 6-inch intervals)
.2875 ÷ 7 = .04107 (dimensional drop for each 6 inches)
```

It is now an easy matter to plot the approximate diameter of the blank over the 15 inches on which the handle assembly will be built. Round off the .04107-inch dimensional drop to .041 and proceed as follows:

```
   .6000 (butt end)
 −.0411
   .5589 (diameter 6 inches from butt)
 −.0411
   .5178 (diameter 12 inches from butt)
 −.0411
   .4767 (diameter 18 inches from butt)
```

If you need to know the diameter at 15 inches from the butt, you interpolate between the 12-inch point and the 18-inch point. Diameter at 12 inches is .5178 less .0206 (one-half the dimensional drop for 6 inches) = .4972 inch. You can now plot this horizontally to match up with your sketch of the handle assembly:

Butt	6″	12″	15″	18″		Midpoint
.600	.5589	.5178	.4972	.4767		.3125

Perhaps for the perfectionist we should note here that the figures we have arrived at, for the diameter of the blank at the above points, will not necessarily be exactly the figures obtained if we measured the blank with a micrometer. One obvious reason is that the taper of the blank may not proceed in even increments from the butt to the midsection. However, our figures are for a relatively short section—the handle assembly—and are adequate for our purposes of determining sizes of the parts we need to order.

Equipped now with a sketch of your design, the parts required, and the approximate sizes, you can proceed with the task of ordering. Some suggestions to keep in mind follow.

Reel seat for spinning and fly rods. Select an outside diameter that is comfortable to your hand (on spinning rods) and large enough to accommodate your reel. Refer to your sketch for the location of the reel seat to see if there is enough clearance between the inside diameter of the seat and the blank to permit installing the bushing. Sometimes you will find that the space is so small that you would have to file the bushing too thin to be workable. In that case go to the next-larger-size reel seat. The outside diameter of the bushing should fit the inside diameter of the seat. You will have to file the inside of the bushing to fit the taper of the blank, so the inside diameter of the bushing should be a little smaller than the blank to assure a tight fit. If the only bushing you can locate to fit properly inside your reel seat is a little too big for the blank, consider winding string or masking tape on the blank to fill the space. Also, figure out the number of bushings or arbors you will need to match the length of the reel seat. It is a good idea to order an extra bushing to allow for mistakes in fitting the parts.

If your fly-rod design calls for a detachable fighting butt, you will need either a special reel seat that comes with the matched, removable butt assembly, or a reel seat with a matching male ferrule around which you will build your own detachable butt. The latter is generally listed in catalogs under "Trolling Reel Seats" or "Heavy-Duty Reel Seats."

Reel seat on boat rods. When using a wood handle, the inside diameter of the reel seat must fit the outside diameter of the turned male wood plug portion on the handle. If the wood plug is too small, order a bushing to fit the inside diameter of the reel seat and file the inside of the bushing to fit the wood plug. The other end of the reel seat usually comes with a matching male ferrule. If not, you will have to order a male ferrule which fits for attachment to the foregrip.

Casting-rod handle and butt ferrule. Since the butt ferrule in this type of rod must fit into the handle, order the handle and ferrule in a matched set whenever possible. You must, of course, make sure that the inside tube diameter of the butt ferrule will fit the butt diameter of your blank. If you are not ordering a matched set, you must pay careful attention to the butt ferrule so that it both fits the blank *and* the built-in ferrule or collet chuck of the handle. If necessary, a plastic collet or fiber reducing bushing can be utilized to effect a tight fit. Regardless of the parts used, it is good insurance to strengthen the rod by gluing a short wood dowel (3 to 5 inches long) inside the hollow glass blank where the butt ferrule is attached.

Grips. If you are using preformed grips, check to see that the outside diameter is the size you want. The inside diameter should be a little smaller than the smallest diameter of the blank section to be covered, so that you can file for a solid fit. The length of the grip should conform to your design. Depending upon shape, it may be feasible to shorten the grip.

When using cork rings to build your own grip, you need to give the same attention to inside and outside diameters. Since the cork rings after mounting will need to be sanded down for a smooth, level surface, it is advisable to order rings with a slightly larger outside diameter than your finished design calls for. When planning a rod that will use sliding metal rings over cork to mount the reel, the grip must be flared out to a larger diameter at each end to prevent the rings from sliding off. Therefore, you need cork rings with a larger outside diameter than the metal rings. The main section of the grip will then be sanded down to the proper diameter to accommodate the metal rings. So, in ordering correct sizes for these parts, both the rings and the corks must be coordinated. Determine also the number of cork rings you need for the length of your grips—and order a few extra.

Winding check. Your sketch indicates the approximate inside diameter for your winding check. These are sold in 64ths, so consult the Conversion Table. If in doubt, order a size smaller and enlarge the hole with a file.

Rod hosel. Again, refer to your sketch for the diameter of the blank where the hosel will be located. The inside diameter of the hosel (at its smallest part) will have to match closely the size of the blank. You cannot enlarge the center hole in some thin hosels by very much, instead you may have to fill the small space with string and glue. Note also the outside diameter of the hosel at its widest, since you will have to taper the cork foregrip to that dimension for a smooth appearance.

Butt cap. In working out your design you will have decided on either a flush-mounted or slip-over cap. The outside diameter is your important dimension if the mount is to be flush with the grip. On a slip-over cap you will need to order one whose inside diameter will fit over the outside of your grip. If you are using a butt plate or a flat disk with a screw in the center, make sure the diameter of the disk matches the outside diameter of the end of your grip.

Tip-top. This obviously has to be the same size as the tip of your blank. If it is a shade too large, you can wind the tip with thread to take up the space. Never—I repeat, never—sand down the tip to fit inside the tube of the tip-top. The wall is exceptionally thin here and you will dangerously weaken the rod at a very crucial point. If ordering guides in a set, be sure to check the tip-top size to see if it fits your blank. On spinning rods especially, I prefer to order the guides individually, since the butt guides are often too small in matched sets.

Guides. If you have not already decided on the kind, number, and sizes of the guides for your rod, it may help to refer back to the discussion and lists at the end of Chapter 3.

Rod ferrules. The female or socket ferrule goes on that section of the blank closest to the butt. Anodized-aluminum ferrules have a dimensional drop—that is, the inside diameter (which fits over the blank) is slightly larger than the corresponding inside diameter of the male ferrule. Order by the hole size in the female or socket section of the ferrule. You get this dimension from your sketch. You may get a better understanding of this by consulting the next chapter, on construction details. When ordering ferrules, always buy an extra rubber O-ring for the male section. Then you will have the correct size if you ever need a replacement in the future.

A final consideration in ordering the parts that will make up your rod: color coordination. Note carefully the colors in which the various parts you have selected are available. On some, you, of course, have no choice. Others are made in a number of colors, or even color combinations. If you do not plan ahead at this stage, your finished rod may end up looking more like a hodgepodge of parts thrown together than an artfully constructed custom rod.

Start by checking the color of the blank and try to have your other parts harmonize with it. All metal fittings and trim should generally be of the same finish. For example, if the ferrules are gold anodized aluminum, order the winding check and probably the reel seat in the same color. You might use a different-finish reel seat, but only if you can tie it to other colors in the completed rod. If the ferrules simply will not match the other metal fittings on the rod, consider covering them completely with a thread wrap.

Each of us has his own ideas of what colors look well together, and what constitutes beauty in a rod. I would suggest, however, that you attempt to develop a basic color theme throughout. An attractive rod generally consists of one or two complementary colors with perhaps just a small accent or two. Your basic colors will, of necessity, have to be built around the blank and the reel seat. If bright colors really turn you on, you have a rainbow array to pick from in guide-wrapping thread. On the other hand, if you want a muted rod composed of earthy warm browns and tans, that certainly can be yours. Just give it some thought—the finished product will be well worth it.

ROD DESIGN SKETCH AND MATERIALS LIST

In the last chapter we discussed the use of a simple design sketch for your working drawing. An example of a sketch for a 7-foot one-handed spinning rod was given.

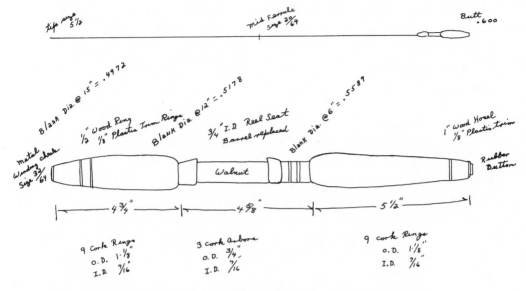

Design sketch with all components indicated for ease in ordering.

This same sketch is now used to determine the individual items that will be needed. By referring to the sketch we can easily calculate the sizes of the various components. As each item is determined, write it along with its size on the sketch. A sample of the now completed sketch is included.

Using this working drawing, a complete materials list is made. The items on this list are then ordered from a catalog, or in some instances, secured locally.

MATERIALS LIST

7' Spinning Rod

Blank: Model # _____, color gold, mid ferrule installed
Wrapping thread: nylon Size A
                 Colors: brown, white, black
Tip-top: Carboloy spinning, Size 5½

Guides: braced spinning, Size 30mm; foulproof, Size $\frac{3}{4}''$, $\frac{1}{2}''$, $\frac{3}{8}''$, $\frac{5}{16}''$, and $\frac{1}{4}''$

Color preserver

Varnish

Anodized-aluminum double-locking spinning reel seat, Size $\frac{3}{4}''$ I.D., color gold

Anodized-aluminum winding check, Size $\frac{32}{64}''$, color gold

20 specie cork rings, $\frac{1}{2}''$ long, Size O.D. $1\frac{1}{8}''$–I.D. $\frac{7}{16}''$

Walnut, $\frac{1}{2}''$ thick (for rings and hosel)

White plastic, $\frac{1}{8}''$ thick (for trim rings)

Walnut reel-seat insert, $2\frac{1}{8}''$ long $\times$ $\frac{13}{16}''$ O.D.

CONVERSION TABLE

Fractions	Inches
$\frac{7}{8}$	.875
$\frac{9}{16}$	.5625
$\frac{10}{16}$	.625
$\frac{11}{16}$	.6875
$\frac{12}{16}$	.750
$\frac{13}{16}$	.8125
$\frac{14}{16}$	.875
$\frac{15}{16}$	.9375
$1\frac{1}{8}$	1.125

CONVERSION TABLE

64ths	Inches	Common fractions
1/64	.015625	
20	.3125	
21	.32813	
22	.34375	
23	.35938	
24	.375	3/8
25	.39063	
26	.40625	
27	.421875	
28	.4375	7/16
29	.45313	
30	.46875	
31	.48438	
32	.500	1/2
33	.51563	
34	.53125	
35	.54688	
36	.5625	9/16
37	.57813	
38	.59375	
39	.60938	
40	.625	5/8
41	.64063	
42	.65625	
43	.67188	
44	.6875	11/16

6. Construction Details

We now get to the actual construction of the rod. You have worked out your design and have all the necessary parts.

One word of caution. Other than installing ferrules and aligning the rod, the work on the handle assembly always progresses from the butt end toward the tip. This was discussed under the basic assembly of the different types of rods in Chapter 3. For example, on a spinning rod you would first fit and glue the rear grip and butt cap, then the bushings and reel seat, and finally the foregrip and winding check or hosel—in that order.

The assembly of each of the parts will be dealt with separately for your easy reference to those jobs applicable to making your rod. Those of you who are particularly handy with tools and have access to the more sophisticated power equipment may well be able to do certain jobs a little differently. However, I strongly suggest you read and study each section before starting. For those who are inexperienced with tools (as I was), follow the procedure carefully and you should have no trouble at all. In fact, your confidence will build rapidly—and you will really enjoy yourself.

GLUING

Many of the various parts are held together with waterproof glue. It is very important that whatever kind of glue you use, you always allow it to dry completely and the bond to cure thoroughly before going on to the next step. Different types and formulas of glue require varying amounts of time to cure. Always read the directions on the container carefully. If they are vague, allow extra time. The future life of your rod depends to a great extent on good solid glue joints. Take your time at the construction stage, and you will never have future problems.

INSTALLING METAL FERRULES

If you are ordering from a catalog and want to place your ferrule at other than the midpoint of the blank, and want to cut the blank yourself, it will probably be necessary to have the blank shipped to you by express. In order to save money on shipping, the mail-order house may agree to cut the blank at the point you desire and include a ferrule of the proper size to fit the blank at the cut. In this day of discount prices, the dealer is certainly entitled to charge you for this extra service, but you will still save money over the express shipping charges.

If you will be cutting the blank yourself, order a ferrule of the size needed for the point on the blank where it will be installed. Exact position usually is not critical, and you can estimate the size. If you have the blank before you order the ferrule, you can, of course, measure the blank with calipers or a micrometer to determine the size.

Now, with both uncut blank and ferrule in hand, slip the female (socket) ferrule over the blank and slide it down to the point where it fits tight. If your ferrule happens to have a portion inside, it can be

Slide female ferrule over uncut blank and mark blank where bottom of ferrule is tight.

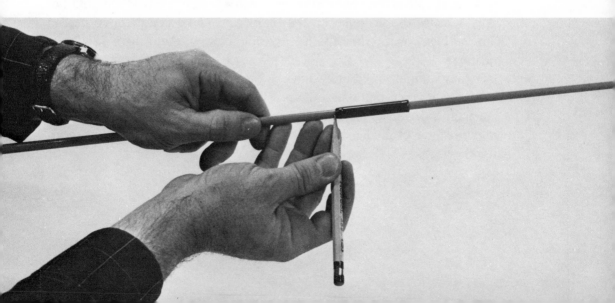

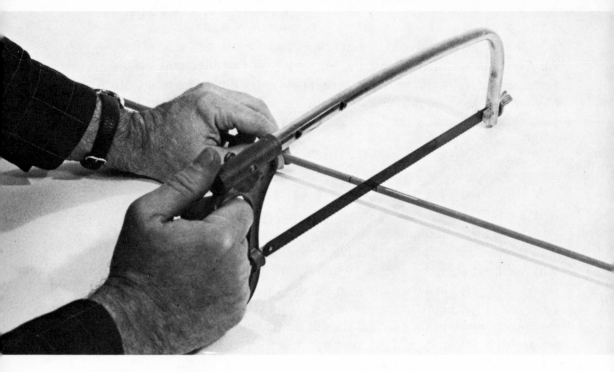

After measuring distance above first mark (see text), cut blank at second mark.

knocked out with a punch. Make a mark around the blank at the bottom of the ferrule. This is where the bottom of the ferrule will be seated when it is glued to the blank.

To determine where, above this mark, to cut the blank, proceed as follows. First, measure the length of the slide (or plug) section of the male ferrule that will fit inside the female ferrule. Add $\frac{1}{8}$ inch to this figure and subtract the total from the length of the female ferrule. This figure is the distance above your first mark where the blank should be cut. Measure the distance on the blank and make your second mark. Cut the blank with a fine-tooth saw such as an X-Acto razor saw or a hack saw.

An example may help. Suppose the length of your female ferrule is $2\frac{1}{2}$ inches and the length of the slide portion of the male ferrule is $1\frac{1}{4}$ inches. Then: $1\frac{1}{4}$ plus $\frac{1}{8}$ equals $1\frac{3}{8}$. Measure $1\frac{3}{8}$ inches from your first mark on the blank, toward the tip, and make your second mark.

The reason you make the cut a little above the point on the blank which measures exactly the inside diameter of the female (socket) ferrule is that the blank has a taper and the inside diameter of the ferrule is straight. The diagrams will help you visualize this. The strength of your blank is concentrated in the outer walls, which are composed of the longitudinal glass fibers. Obviously, you do not want to remove any more of the outer material than is necessary. So if you plan your cut so that the fit of the blank is snug at the end of the ferrule away from the cut (point A), sanding of the blank at that point is reduced to a minimum. It is true that the surface of the blank does have a coating which can be removed without affecting strength, but it is best to play

Installing a metal ferrule. The female ferrule is glued on the butt section. The cut end (B) can be covered with short lengths of thread to fill out the space. The cut end of the tip section (C) can be sanded for a tight fit inside the male ferrule.

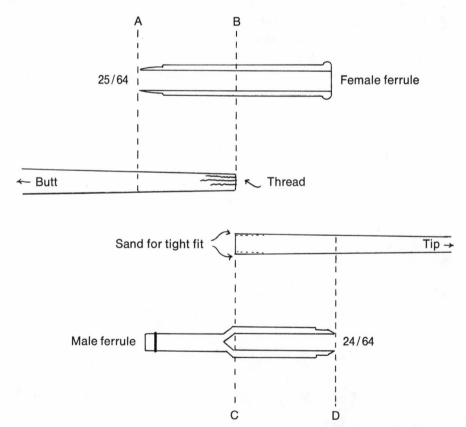

it safe and not have to remove any more material than necessary. The cut end of the blank which fits inside the ferrule (point B) can be filled out with a few short lengths of thread laid over the cut longitudinally along the blank.

There is a dimensional drop between the inside diameters of the female and male ferrules. The inside diameter of the male ferrule is slightly smaller, since it goes on the tip end of the blank. On the Featherweight brand of ferrules, for example, this difference or drop is .010 inch on ferrules size $\frac{11}{64}$ through $\frac{16}{64}$. On size $\frac{17}{64}$ through $\frac{43}{64}$ it is $\frac{1}{64}$ or .015625 inch. The purpose of this "drop" is to better accommodate the end of the tip section of the blank, since it has tapered to a smaller diameter than the bottom end of the female ferrule. To fit the end of the tip section of the blank into the male ferrule, a small amount of sanding on the cut end is generally necessary (point C). Since this portion of the blank is placed the deepest into the ferrule, any slight loss of strength there will have no effect on the strength of the rod. Depending upon the taper of some blanks, too much sanding of the end of the blank may be required for a fit. In that case, cut off a small portion of the end of the blank. In rare situations you may have to remove an inch or more. However, cut off small pieces at

Apply liquid thermoplastic ferrule cement to blank.

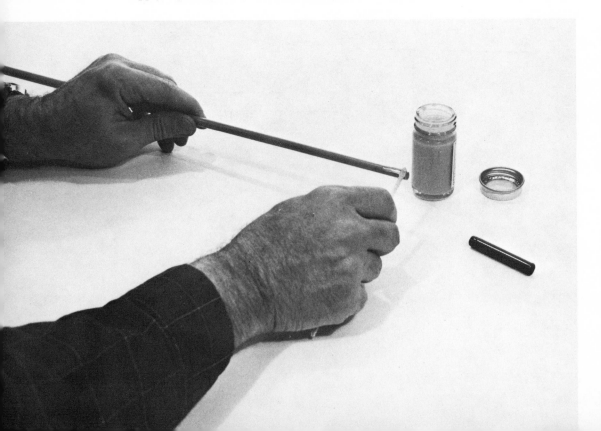

a time, such as ⅛ inch to ¼ inch, sand the end and test for fit. Using this procedure, the fit at the upper end of the male ferrule (point D) will be tight with no sanding there, and no loss of strength.

Work slowly and constantly check your fit by testing. When the male ferrule will slide over the end of the tip section, make a mark on the blank at the upper end of the ferrule. This mark and the one on the butt section will serve as guides when you apply the glue. Use a good thermoplastic ferrule cement if you want to be able to remove the ferrule in the future for replacement repairs. You can use either the liquid or stick form. Apply the cement and slip on the ferrules. Heat the ferrule over a flame so that the cement flows throughout the joint for a strong bond. After the ferrules have cooled, carefully trim off any excess cement that was squeezed out of the joints with a razor blade.

Installation of butt ferrules for use on casting and spin-cast rods follows essentially the same procedure. Remove the minimum of material from the extreme end of the blank to create a solid fit into the barrel of the ferrule. Work by sanding progressively from the very end, back up the blank, constantly checking the fit. As mentioned before, glue a tapered dowel 3 to 5 inches long inside the glass blank for extra strength.

Heat ferrule so that cement flows throughout joint for a strong bond.

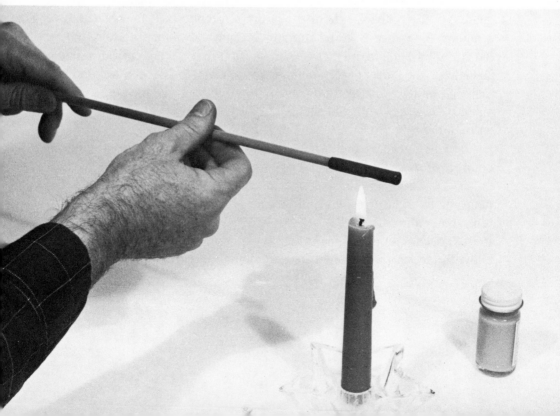

MAKING GLASS FERRULES

If you prefer a glass-to-glass ferrule, you can make one of the glass-plug type from a piece of solid fiberglass blank (the strongest), or a hollow fiberglass blank. Essentially, what you do is fit a glass plug, or ferrule, to the inside of the hollow glass blank of each section to be joined and glue the plug into the butt section. The walls surrounding the plug are reinforced with thread wrappings and a coat of epoxy or fiberglass resin. "Boots" Voigt has been using this type of ferrule, when requested by his customers, and his fly rods and spinning rods have held up to the wild thrashings of 100-pound-plus tarpon. From personal experience, that is about as tough a test as you can give a rod.

As with any ferrule, you first decide on the location. I prefer a bit lower on the butt section than the midpoint of the blank. This provides a longer section of uninterrupted bending before the resistance of the ferrule is met, as mentioned before. Also, with a glass ferrule, it places the stress point at a slightly stronger part of the rod.

I am in the habit of working with an uncut blank, but if your blank has already been cut, you can adjust the directions. The construction steps can be followed on the accompanying diagrams. First mark the intended cut with a grease pencil or a soft lead pencil. With the blank still intact, wrap rod-winding thread (in the same manner as wrapping guides) firmly on each side of the point of intended cut for about 1½ to 2 inches. These two wraps should be separated in the middle, where the cut will be made, by ⅜ to ¼ inch. Next make an overwrap starting flush with the edge of the underwrap closest to the center, and extending one-half to two-thirds of the length of the underwrap. You can make both wraps with the same-size thread, but the overwrap will lay on better if it is of slightly heavier thread.

Do not yet cut the blank. Give the wraps a couple of coats of color preserver. When dry, coat the wraps with a strong, durable finish. This could be a couple of coats of clear epoxy (two-solution) paint, or fiberglass resin. Apply either with a small flat brush and extend the coating about ⅛ inch beyond the end of each wrap and over the exposed section of blank in the middle. Set the blank aside and allow the finish to dry and cure completely.

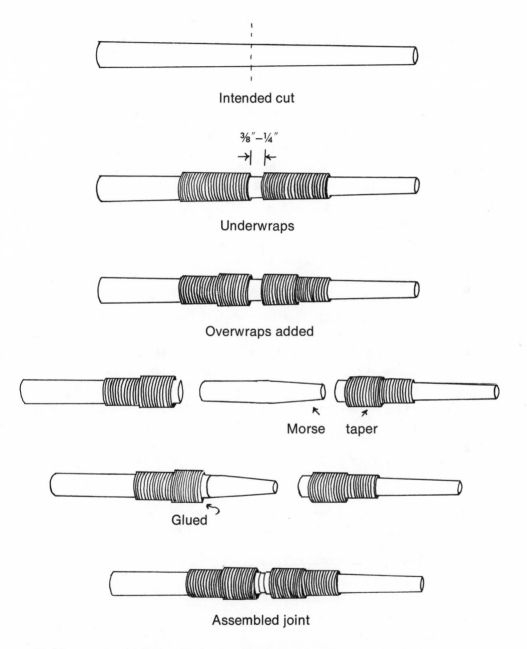

Intended cut

⅜"–¼"

Underwraps

Overwraps added

Morse   taper

Glued

Assembled joint

Making a glass ferrule. Position of ferrule is marked, and underwraps are made on each side. Overwraps are added, and blank is cut. Glass plug is fitted to both sections, then glued to butt section.

Use a fine-tooth saw to make as straight a cut as possible, and "debur" the cut edges with fine sandpaper. Do not cut the blank in the exact center of the two wrappings. Instead, offset it slightly so that the remaining length of the blank on the tip end (which will become the socket or female ferrule) is a bit longer than the exposed blank on the butt end (which will become the male ferrule). The reason for this is to allow future adjustments. We discussed earlier the fact that glass-to-glass joints tend to loosen in time. If and when this occurs on your rod, you can carefully file away a bit of the exposed blank on the tip (female) section of the joint. This will then enable you to push the taper inside the hollow glass blank farther onto the glass plug, once again tightening the joint.

With the blank cut you are now ready to fashion and fit the glass plug. The strongest material is solid fiberglass, and it should be used on heavy-duty rods. On average or light rods you can use a plug made of hollow fiberglass. If the former is unavailable, your best source is a cheap solid-glass blank or an old discarded or broken rod. The most important consideration is that the taper of the plug be as similar as possible to the taper of your blank. This will greatly simplify the fitting job if you are using solid fiberglass, and is a necessity for hollow fiberglass where there is little room for fitting without seriously weakening the plug.

The most critical fit will be on the tip section. This is where your

A properly fitted "morse taper" provides an excellent friction seal and stress distribution. A poorly fitted plug causes unequal stress distribution.

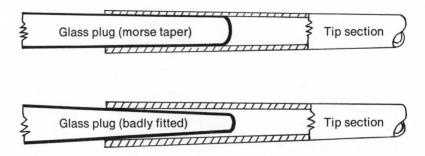

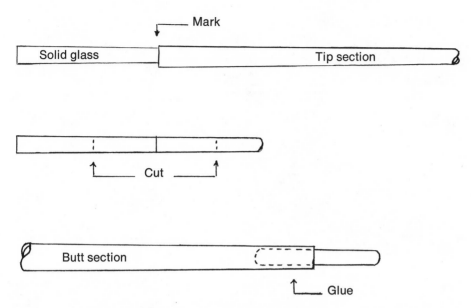

Fitting is simplified when the taper of the solid-glass plug matches the taper of the hollow blank. The tapered plug is inserted into tip section for a tight fit, and then marked. The plug is cut, rammed into position in the butt section, and glued.

hollow-glass blank will slip on and off the plug. If the tip end of the plug fits perfectly inside the hollow-glass tip section of your blank, you will have a "morse taper" and a good friction lock. The best way to determine this is to insert your length of plug material into the bottom end of the tip section of your blank. Do not ram it in tight, but carefully push it into the hollow tip section until you feel a tight fit. Now check for wobble—there should be none. If your tapers match, you may not have to do any further fitting of the tip section.

If there is a wobble of the plug inside the blank, make a temporary pencil mark encircling the plug at the point it meets or enters the blank. Now, remove the plug and carefully reduce its diameter a bit on the lower or butt end, just below *and* around your pencil line. Do this by scraping with a sharp knife held at a 90-degree angle to the plug. Do not "whittle" the plug by cutting into it with the knife blade. Always scrape. Make a couple passes with the knife, then rotate the

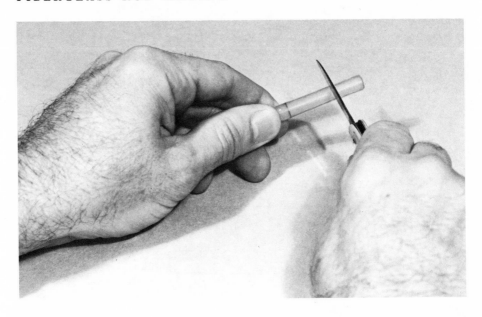

Scraping the glass plug to correct the taper.

plug a few degrees and make a couple more passes. Keep repeating until you have made one complete revolution. Reinsert the plug into the tip section of the blank and again test the fit. Keep repeating this procedure until you have a perfect fit. You can use fine sandpaper to remove the last bit of material.

When you are satisfied with the fit, mark the plug with a pencil line where it meets and enters the tip section of your blank. Remove the plug and cut it off about 1½ inches above your pencil mark — toward the tip. Make the cut square and round off the cut edge with fine sandpaper.

If at the start of this fitting operation you found that your plug material would not quite fit into the open end of the tip section of your blank, you can still effect a fit if the plug is of solid fiberglass. Use the scraping technique to reduce the diameter of the plug over about a 1½-inch length. Work slowly and carefully, since the fit is critical. If your plug material is of hollow fiberglass and will not fit into the blank, you cannot shape it since it will become too weak. You need a thinner piece of hollow fiberglass or a solid piece.

Now that you have the tip section fitted, you can turn your attention to the butt section. Here the plug will ultimately be glued into place, so the fit is not as critical. The film of glue will fill any small space. Cut off the plug about 1½ inches below your pencil mark (toward the butt) and round the cut edge with fine sandpaper.

To fit this portion of the plug, you can simply reduce the diameter of the very end so that it will just slide into the upper opening in the butt section of your blank. While this will not be a perfect fit, the glue will fill the space and provide a strong joint. The previously discussed scraping technique is used.

If you want a tighter fit (which really is not necessary), you can insert the plug from the *bottom* end of the butt section. You will need a long dowel or rod of some sort to push it into position. It should fit inside your blank so that the pencil mark on the plug sticks out about ⅛ inch. Fitting is again accomplished by the scraping technique.

With the plug now fitted to both sections of the blank, you can glue it into the butt section. Use epoxy glue and coat both the lower portion of the plug and the inside of the butt section of the blank. Insert the plug into position in the blank and carefully wipe off any excess glue. Make sure there is no glue remaining on the projecting section of the plug or the blank. Set aside until the epoxy has thoroughly cured.

If solid fiberglass is not available for the plug, you can make one that is almost as good from a dowel of Plexiglas (acrylic). This is available from plastics dealers (check the Yellow Pages of your telephone directory under "Plastics") or hobby and craft stores. The disadvantages of this material are that it is not made up of glass fibers and is only available in dowels of constant diameter. You will have to do more shaping to effect a perfect fit.

If you want to build a glass-plug ferrule for a blank that has already been cut, do the above steps in the same order. Wrap and coat the ends of the sections to be joined first, then fit and glue the plug.

When assembling your completed rod for fishing, join the sections the same as with any glass-to-glass ferrule—with a twisting motion. Place the two sections together so that their alignment is off by about 90°. Then, twist the sections into proper alignment while pushing them together. The same twisting motion is used in disassembling the sections.

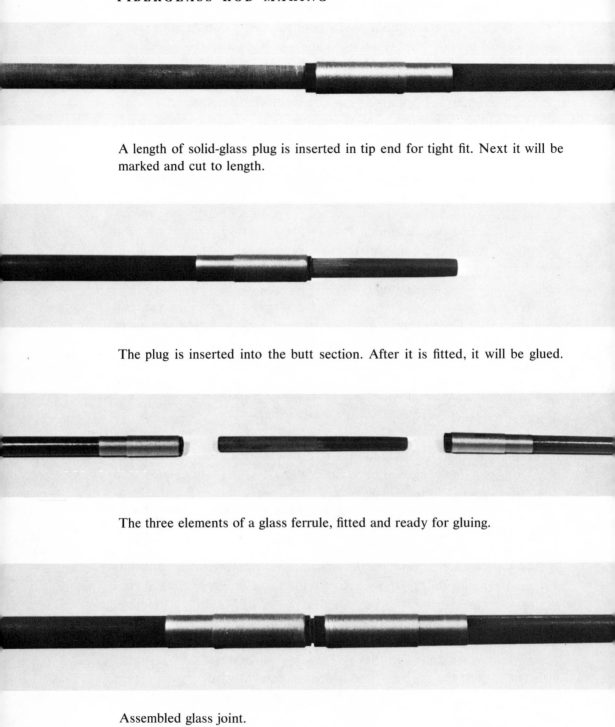

A length of solid-glass plug is inserted in tip end for tight fit. Next it will be marked and cut to length.

The plug is inserted into the butt section. After it is fitted, it will be glued.

The three elements of a glass ferrule, fitted and ready for gluing.

Assembled glass joint.

Rolling the blank to locate the "high side" or spline.

ALIGNING THE BLANK

Most fiberglass blanks will not flex exactly evenly in any direction. There generally is a spline or "high side" — a position in which the blank has slightly more power. This side should be located after the rod ferrules are installed and the adhesive has cured. Later, the guides will be wrapped on the side *opposite* the high side.

To find the high side, position the blank at about a 45° angle. Rest the butt on a smooth flat surface and support the tip section from beneath with the open palm of the left hand. With the fingers of the right hand press down in the middle of the blank, bending it slightly, and roll it back and forth. The high side will be found where the rod tends to "jump" under your fingers. Mark the side *opposite* the high side. Repeat the procedure a few times to check yourself.

Sometimes the high side is not very pronounced and you will have difficulty locating it. In that case, proceed as follows. With the rod sections joined together, hold the blank up to eye level and sight along the blank to see if the tip goes off at an angle. If it does, turn the tip section (by rotating the male ferrule inside the female ferrule) a bit at a time

Blank bends in this direction ↑

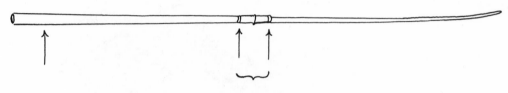

Mark ferrules on this side

For fixed reel sear, install fixed hood on this side   Install guides on this side

Aligning the blank.

until you get the straightest possible configuration. You probably will not be able to eliminate the curve completely. This is not a problem because you will install the guides on the side *opposite* the bend, thereby straightening the blank.

It will now be necessary to mark the ferrules on the side of the blank *opposite* the curve for future reference. You will need to locate this side when you install a fixed reel seat and again when you wrap on the guides. Sight along the aligned blank and first mark each ferrule with a soft lead pencil, crayon, or grease pencil. A more permanent mark is then made very lightly with a center punch or nail on the rim of each ferrule. Hereafter, you will always be able to join the sections of the blank in exactly the same position, knowing that the marks are on the side where the guides (and the hood on a fixed reel seat) will be located.

In the manufacture of commercial rods this step is sometimes skipped, or done improperly, and a rod that is an abomination to cast is the result. This is another example of why a carefully fitted custom-made rod will almost always be superior to a commercial rod.

FITTING BUSHINGS, ARBORS, AND GRIPS

The bushing or arbor which fits under the reel seat must have its straight inside diameter reshaped to fit the taper of that section of the blank which it covers. This is done by careful filing and sanding.

The first step is to mark on the blank the length which will be covered by the bushing. The easiest way to accomplish this is to slip the reel seat over the blank, place it in the proper position according to your design sketch, and use it as a template to mark a circle around the blank at each end. Remove the reel seat. Next, cut the bushing to the proper length to fit inside the reel seat. If you are using cork arbors you will have to use the correct number and possibly shorten one of them. I suggest you plainly mark the outside of individual short arbors #1, #2, #3, etc. so that you can keep track of their order as each is fitted to the blank. Also, mark one end of each arbor to indicate that it is to be placed toward the butt end of the taper. When using only one bushing, large enough to accommodate the length of the reel seat, mark one end to indicate the butt end. These marks will be covered when the rod is assembled, so they can be made with a fiber-tipped marker or ball-point pen.

Your objective in filing and sanding the inside of a bushing or, for that matter, a preassembled grip, is twofold: to remove more material from inside one end than the other so as to fit the taper, and to remove the material evenly around the inside so the bushing will be centered on the blank. The easiest way to do this is to mark the edge of the bushing as a reference point as you turn and file. Do not try to scrape away much at one time. Instead work slowly, removing only small amounts.

The procedure I use for fitting both bushings and grips is as follows. Lay the bushing on a flat level surface such as a workbench or table, with the end of the bushing at the front edge. Insert the file into the inside at a very slight angle (approximating that of the blank taper) so that the file, when moved in and out, will press more on the end of the bushing toward you than on the opposite end. In other words, you want to remove a bit more material from the front inside (the butt end) than the rear inside. Stroke the file in and out with light pressure

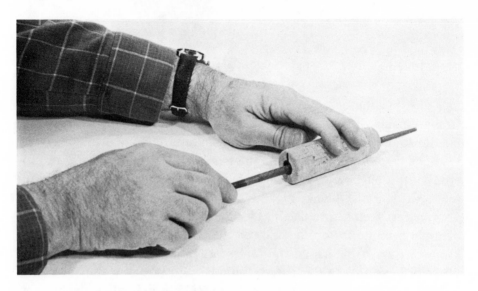

Filing a grip. Note the reference mark to aid in making the same number of file strokes for each 1/8 turn of the grip.

applied directly down toward the table. Make a given number of strokes — perhaps four or eight, depending upon the amount of material to be removed. Then, using the mark on the edge of the bushing as a reference, turn the bushing $\frac{1}{8}$ turn. Again file with pressure applied straight down for the same number of strokes, then turn the bushing $\frac{1}{8}$ turn. Proceed in this manner until you have completely rotated the bushing one full turn. Check for fit on the blank. Keep repeating this process until you approach the proper fit. Your file will be thicker, or have a wider diameter, at its handle end. This assists you in removing more material from one end. Depending upon how much you must enlarge the inside hole in the entire bushing, you may have to reverse the bushing on the table end for end, and file some from the inside of both ends. When you periodically check the fit, determine if there is any wobble at either end. If there is, it indicates you are removing too much material from that end in proportion to the taper. If both ends wobble, the center is still too thick.

As you approach the fit of bushing to blank, halve the number of strokes with the file for each $\frac{1}{8}$ rotation. If the bushing is very long, you may develop a high spot, or thicker interior section, somewhere near the middle of the bushing, as you proceed. This can best be removed with a length of wood dowel wrapped with coarse sandpaper.

When using the dowel, rotate the bushing every few strokes as you did with the file. The removal of the last bit of material from the inside of the bushing should be performed with the dowel.

Throughout the process the best technique is to work slowly. Remove small amounts, and keep checking the fit by sliding the bushing down over the blank from the tip end. When the bushing slides firmly without any pressure into the correct position you have marked on the blank — stop sanding.

Now, check the fit of the bushing over its length. It does not have to fit precisely all along its length, since the glue used will fill very small spaces. However, if you detect a distinct wobble of the bushing on the blank at one end, you need to make some adjustments. This is done by wrapping a small section of the blank where the wobble occurs (and the inside diameter of the bushing is now too large) with thread, string, or masking tape. The thickness of the filler selected will depend upon the size of the space to be filled.

Wrap the string or thread tightly around the blank, using the same technique as for wrapping on guides. Check the fit of the bushing over the blank. If the wrapped area is a little too tight (too thick), you can either rewrap with lighter string (the safest course), or carefully remove a slight bit more from the inside of the bushing.

When you have the proper fit, coat the blank section over which the bushing fits with glue. A length of pipe cleaner dipped into the glue makes a fine disposable applicator. Slip the bushing over the blank and into place. Wipe off any excess glue that was squeezed out in joining the parts, and allow to dry completely. If the fit before gluing is a little loose, you may want to coat not only the blank with glue, but the inside of the bushing as well. Here the pipe cleaner is ideal. Be careful when slipping the coated bushing down over the blank and into place. Any glue that gets on the blank can generally be cleaned off if wiped immediately with a cloth dampened with alcohol. Lay the blank in a horizontal position balanced on two points other than the bushing, and allow the glue to dry thoroughly.

INSTALLING THE REEL SEAT

After an adequate amount of time has elapsed for the cement you are using to cure into a solid bond, you are ready to fit and install the reel seat. Actually very little fitting should be necessary, since the outside diameter of the bushing you used should have been selected to fit the inside diameter of the reel seat. Light sanding and truing so that the reel seat slides over the bushing is generally all that is necessary. Sometimes when using short cork arbors, not quite enough material was removed from the inside of one of them. Consequently, the arbor was more or less forced into position, swelling the outside. It will have to be sanded down for a smooth fit into the reel seat. The best way to sand this down without inadvertently reducing the outside diameter of other arbors is with sandpaper glued or held on a flat stick. An emery board does a good job. Sand parallel to the blank, keeping the board flat, and rotate the blank a bit at a time until the arbors are all even.

Coat the outside of the arbors with glue and slide the reel seat into place. If the fit was loose, also coat the inside of the reel-seat tube with a pipe cleaner dipped into glue. Observe the same caution when slipping a coated reel seat down over the blank as you did with the bushing. Immediately clean off any glue on the blank. Note: The final position of a fixed reel seat must be on a direct line with the planned position of the guides. As discussed above under the head "Aligning the Blank," the rod must be properly aligned and the guides installed on the opposite side of the bend in the rod. Check the mark you made on the socket ferrule on the butt section of your blank. While the glue is still wet, twist the reel seat to align it with the mark on the ferrule. Now carefully set it aside to dry in a position so that the seat will not be accidentally moved.

CUSTOMIZING A REEL SEAT

If you have decided to customize your aluminum reel seat with a wood or cork center, you will have to make two cuts through the metal reel seat to remove the center. These cuts should be just behind the fixed hood that holds one reel foot (A) and at the end of the threads (B). Take care to make a straight cut through the tube with a fine-tooth hacksaw. If you are using a fine-tooth power saw, insert a tight-fitting dowel into the barrel. Dress the cut edges with a file, and finish using fine emery cloth or fine sandpaper. The cut-out center of the tube will, of course, be discarded. The two end pieces will be mounted on the blank over bushings or arbors in exactly the manner described pre-

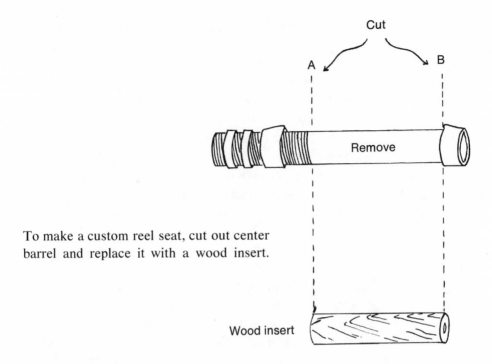

Cut

A   B

Remove

To make a custom reel seat, cut out center barrel and replace it with a wood insert.

Wood insert

viously for mounting the entire reel seat. The only difference is that they will be separated by a length of wood cylinder or cork rings approximately equal in length to the cut-out metal section. The outside diameter of this cylinder must be exactly the same as the section of metal tube removed, allowing the sliding hood to move over it.

It should be mentioned here that you have an opportunity now to adjust the overall length of your reel seat to fit the reels you intend to use. If you plan to use only small reels with a relatively short span over the length of the reel mounting feet, you can, if you desire, shorten the length of the seat. To shorten, make your cut (B) so that you remove some of the threaded section of the barrel, and/or use a shorter section of wood than the length of metal tube you removed. If large reels will be used with a long mounting span and the reel seat was short, you can lengthen the seat by using a longer section of wood than the length of metal removed. I am not suggesting here that you necessarily change the length of the reel seat. In all probability the original length will be adequate in all respects. However, reel-seat length generally varies with the diameter. A slim seat will be short and a thick seat long. If you prefer a thin seat to fit your hand, but want to use it with large reels, you do have that option using this technique.

Returning to the construction, the wood cylinder may have been purchased from a catalog or made by yourself (or perhaps a friend with a lathe). In any event, the diameter of the center hole should be a bit larger than the widest part of the blank over which it will fit. It is much easier to fill this space with string or masking tape to accommodate the blank taper than to hand-file hardwood such as walnut or cherry. So, wrap the blank with string—a bit heavier on the narrow end of the blank. Check the fit. Then saturate the wrapping with glue and slip the wood insert into place.

Another way to make a wood insert for a customized fixed reel seat is to build it up from wood rings. As discussed later in this chapter, these rings are easily made with a hole saw. If you use this method, you may want to consider two different woods which will provide contrast, such as walnut and white wood (poplar). The rings can be alternated or arranged in any pleasing combination. You can use either of two approaches. On one, you first shape the outside diameter of each ring to match the diameter of the removed metal section, and then fit the inside diameter to the blank. After gluing into position, the rings are fine-sanded for a perfect fit. On the other, you glue the rings together and clamp until dry. Then the resulting wood cylinder is turned or sanded to the proper outside diameter on a lathe, or chucked into an electric drill with an arbor. This cylinder is then treated the same as a one-piece wood cylinder, as discussed earlier, for fitting in place on the blank.

Rings of walnut and poplar, cut with a hole saw.

A standard reel seat and a custom seat made from it. Wood rings are alternating walnut and poplar.

An insert made of cork lacks the contrasting beauty of dark wood, but it does provide a better gripping surface for your hand. It is also considerably easier to build and fit to the blank. All you need to do is fashion a short cork grip from cork rings as discussed in the following sections. If you want a dark contrasting color in a cork insert, you may be able to modify a section of a preformed composition, or "burnt-cork," grip.

INSTALLING PREASSEMBLED CORK GRIPS

The preassembled cork grip, be it composition cork or glued cork rings, is fitted to the taper of the blank exactly the same way a bushing is fitted. If you are going to shorten the length of the grip, do it before starting to file. On the other hand, if you are going to make minor modifications to the outside diameter or shape of the grip, do that work after it is glued and permanently bonded into position on the blank.

Because of the shape of the grip, there will probably be no need to mark which end will be placed over the butt end of the rod. However, you will need a mark on the edge as a reference for rotating the grip as you file the inside hole. If the grip is too long to work comfortably, cut it in two parts and fit each section separately. It is much more difficult to file an even taper on a long grip than on two shorter ones. Just make sure your cut is smooth by using a fine-tooth saw. A power saw with a fine blade is a help here, but certainly not necessary. Before making the cut, place a removable mark (soft lead pencil is good) across the point of the intended cut and parallel to the direction of the grip. This

Cutting a preassembled grip.

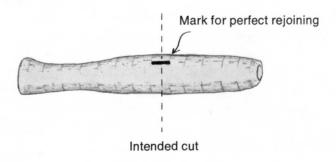

Mark for perfect rejoining

Intended cut

will enable you to align the two parts perfectly when you glue them to the blank and to each other. Light sanding with fine sandpaper after the glue dries will remove any noticeable joint.

Minor modifications to the grip can be made after the glue is completely bonded. If the outside diameter is slightly larger than is comfortable for your hand, it can be reduced with medium sandpaper, then fine. First work back and forth along the length, rotating the grip for evenness. Finish up with a strip of fine sandpaper wrapped around the grip and rotated under your hand. Other small changes in shape can be made depending upon your desires and ability with sandpaper.

BUILDING GRIPS FROM CORK RINGS

Working with cork rings gives you the greatest freedom in designing your grips, allows you to be a creative craftsman, and most of all, is just plain fun. There is a bit of the sculptor buried in all of us, and it is exciting and rewarding to see the finished form emerge as you work. Few other materials can be as easily and rapidly shaped as can cork, using only sandpaper for a tool.

There are three approaches that I have found work well: (1) fitting each ring individually to the blank, then shaping by hand; (2) gluing the rings together to form a tube, which is then fitted and shaped; and (3) gluing the rings together on, but not onto, a tight-fitting dowel for shaping by turning. I will discuss each of them.

The first method of fitting each individual ring to the blank simplifies matching the inside ring diameters to the blank. You do not have to file a long taper, just fit each ½-inch-long piece of cork to the blank beneath it. The rings must be assembled onto the blank in the same order in which they were fitted, so mark the outside diameter of each ring with a number. Start by filing the hole of the first ring until it slides snugly into position, then leave it there and fit your #2 ring and leave it in place on the blank. Continue until all the rings are in place. When filing the rings, observe the same technique of rotation discussed above in the section on fitting bushings to keep the hole centered in the cork. Remove all the rings and glue them one by one onto the blank, and to each other. Coat the blank and each flat face of the rings with glue. Lightly clamping the grip together lengthwise while drying will

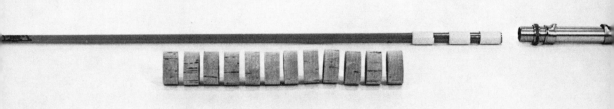

The components for making a fly-rod grip from cork rings. The reel seat will first be glued over the bushings, which are built up from masking tape.

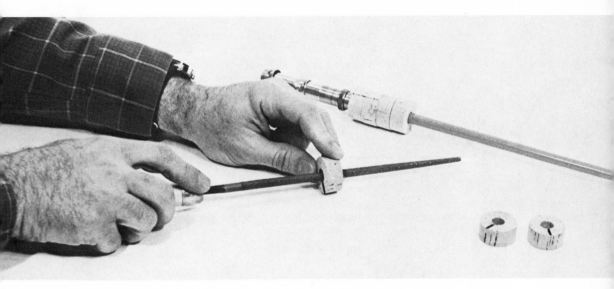

Each cork ring is individually fitted to the blank and left in place, unglued, until all are fitted.

The rings are removed and then glued one by one to the blank and to each other. Keep them in the same order.

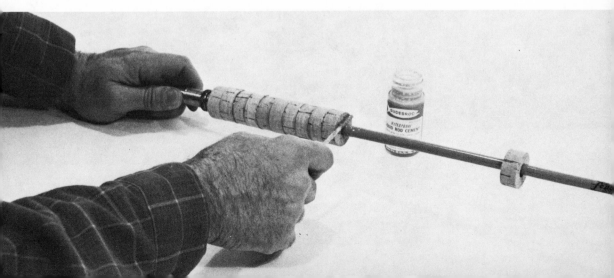

Heavy rubber bands clamp the rings until the glue is dry.

The cork cylinder from which the rings will be hand-sanded.

The basic contour is developed with coarse sandpaper.

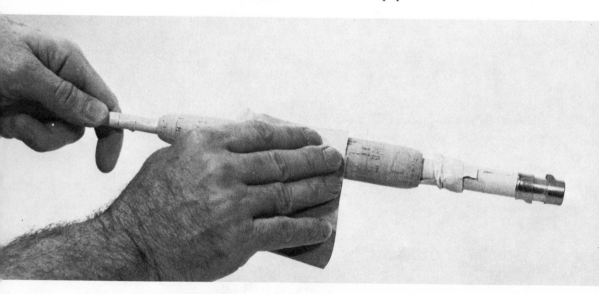

The grip after finishing with very fine sandpaper.

help strengthen it, although it is not absolutely necessary. Any type of clamp that will fit is fine; however, you will need two to maintain even pressure on each side. I have found that heavy rubber bands stretched tightly from end to end work very well. The rubber bands can be held in place with short lengths of dowels, or heavy nails, laid across each end of the grip.

The glue should be completely dry before you begin your shaping operation. Develop the basic contours with medium-coarse sandpaper. Regardless of the hand motion you use in sanding, always make the same number of strokes — about eight — then rotate the blank slightly and repeat until you have worked your way around the grip. Although this seems a bit tedious, it is the best way to keep your grip round and centered. When you sand for too long on one side, you run the risk of forming a flat side on the grip.

Generally you can work entirely free-form. However, if you want to shape your grip to a precise design, it is best to make a simple template or guide. This can be easily cut out of shirt cardboard or similar material. First carefully draw the shape of your design to full scale and then cut out and discard the portion that represents the grip. (See the accompanying diagram.) The resulting outline can be held against the cork periodically to check your progress. As you approach the final contours, use a finer grade of sandpaper. Slightly round off any square edges to prevent the cork from chipping or breaking.

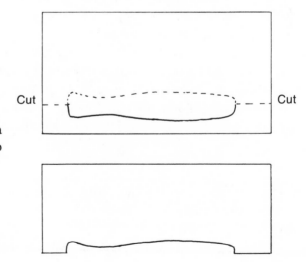

A template for shaping a grip. Draw outline of grip full size.

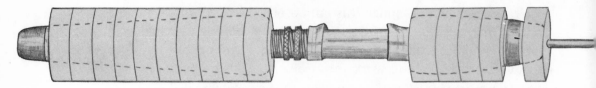

When constructing a grip by fitting and gluing cork rings individually to the blank, first shape trim rings and hosels to finished diameter and glue them into position. When dry, sand cork to a flush fit with trim rings and hosels.

If your design of the grip calls for some inlays of wood rings or other decorative trim, this approach of fitting and gluing each ring separately to the blank works very well. The wood, plastic, etc. should be first shaped to the *exact* finished outside diameter—that is, the diameter it will have in the finished grip. The center hole is then fitted to the diameter of the blank at its proper position among the cork rings, or made slightly larger. If you have made the center hole larger in the trim ring, fill out the center space with string wound on the blank. After gluing the grip together, the larger-diameter cork rings will be sanded down to the same size as the wood rings to form a perfectly flush surface on the grip. (See diagram.)

The second method of making a grip from cork rings is to glue the rings together, forming a tube. The proper number of rings are coated with glue on each side, clamped together, and allowed to dry. Any clamp can be used. A very simple and effective way to hold the rings in position under pressure is to use a long bolt through the center of the tube. Washers are placed on each end of the cork tube and it is drawn up tight with a nut over the bolt. It is also possible sometimes to buy lengths of cork tube made of rings already glued together. The inside diameter of your fabricated cork cylinder is then fitted to the taper of the blank (as discussed above under "Installing Preassembled Cork

When gluing up a cork cylinder, one method is to clamp rings together with a long bolt and washers.

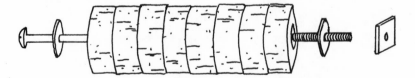

Grips") and glued into position. After the bond has cured, the grip is sanded to shape, using the same technique as outlined in the first method.

The third method, which I like best, is to turn your grip on a lathe, drill press, or hand drill. Today, most of us have electric hand drills, and this method is easy and works very well. Since you need a solid center for turning, select a straight piece of wood dowel with a diameter that will form a very tight fit in the center holes of the cork rings. To test the straightness of a dowel, roll it on a flat surface such as a table top. If the dowel wobbles as it rolls, it is warped or curved. The fit of the cork rings onto the dowel must be tight enough so that the cork does not rotate easily. I wrap the dowel with cotton string first, and then force the corks onto the dowel with a twisting motion in the direction of the wrap. Before each cork is forced onto the dowel and twisted into position, coat both sides of the cork ring—but *not* the center—with glue. Be careful not to get glue on the inside of the center hole, or you will not be able to remove the finished grip from the dowel. Twist each cork ring tightly against the previous one and allow to dry thoroughly.

If you are using a lathe, trim the dowel off flush with the cork at each end. Locate your centers and mount on the lathe. If you are going to use a mounted electric hand drill or a drill press for turning, leave a

Another method of gluing up a cylinder, which permits turning the grip in a lathe or drill chuck. The rings are forced onto a dowel wrapped with string. Avoid getting any glue in the center of the rings.

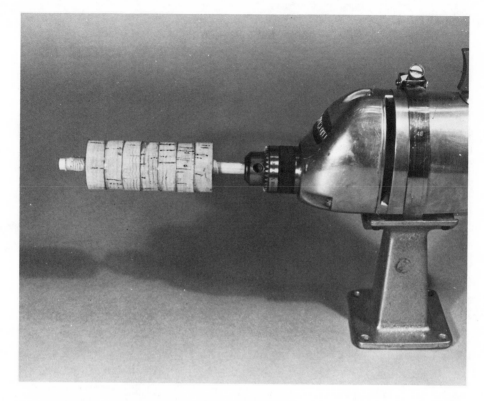

The protruding dowel is chucked into a drill.

sufficient length of dowel protruding from the cork cylinder on one end to mount in the drill chuck. In planning this operation, check to see if the diameter dowel you will have to use with your cork rings will fit inside the chuck of your drill press or hand drill. Occasionally, on large-diameter blanks, where you are using cork rings with large inside diameters, the necessary dowels may be too thick to fit the chuck and you will have to use one of the other methods for forming the grip.

The actual turning is done entirely with strips of medium and fine sandpaper about ½ inch to 1½ inches wide. Hold the sandpaper strips by the ends and lay them across the cork cylinder at a slight angle. It is not necessary to apply much pressure against the cork. In fact, too much pressure can cause the cylinder to come loose from the dowel and not turn. To avoid this use narrow strips of sandpaper, keep the angle of the paper across the cork slight (do not wrap it around), and

106

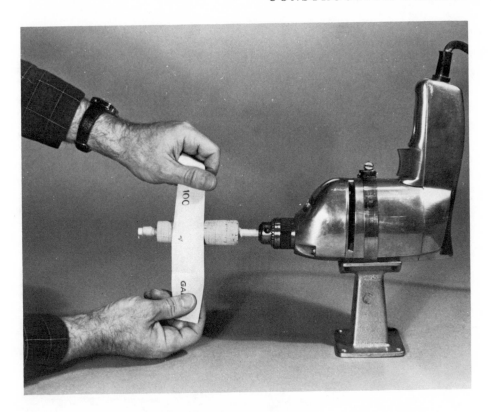

Sandpaper is held across cork at a slight angle.

use only enough pressure to cause the sandpaper to remove cork slowly.

Start with medium sandpaper, not coarse, and first true up the cylinder. Check the diameter with calipers or simple half-circle templates cut out of shirt cardboard to see how much more material must be removed at the thickest section of your grip design. Maintaining a constant-diameter cylinder, sand down to just a bit thicker than that diameter. Now proceed with shaping the grip to your planned configuration. Check your progress often as you remove material, since cork is removed rather quickly. Work free-form, or make one large cardboard template (as discussed under the first method of hand sanding), or a number of half-circle templates of the exact diameters for key points. While working with the medium sandpaper always stop a bit short of the desired finished diameter, then complete your sanding of the entire grip with very fine sandpaper for a smooth surface.

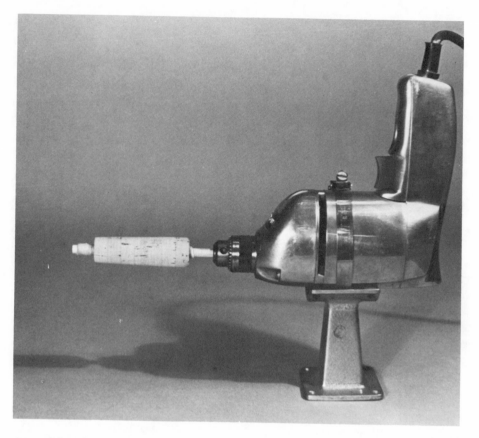

A completed turned grip. If it does not come off the dowel easily, the string can be pulled out to free it.

Remove the completed grip from the lathe or drill, and see if you can carefully work it loose from the center dowel with a twisting motion. Since some of the glue from the corks may have inadvertently gotten on the string, you may encounter some resistance. If you do, do not attempt to force the grip off and risk damage. Instead, use a pin to pick out one end of the string from inside the grip and unravel the string by pulling it out parallel with the dowel. You now have a "preassembled grip" of your own design, which can be fitted in place on your blank as discussed previously.

INSTALLING AND BUILDING GRIPS
FOR METAL SPINNING RINGS

If your design utilizes sliding metal spinning rings to mount your reel, you will have to assemble your grip differently. The rings must be free to slide along the grip, so the outside diameter of the grip must be just slightly smaller than the inside diameter of the rings. The ends of the grip must be flared to prevent the rings from coming off. Therefore, the rings must be installed when the grip is glued to the blank.

Preassembled grips of this type come in two pieces for this purpose. If you form your own grip by turning on a drill or lathe, make it in two sections, flaring one end of each. To obtain the correct diameter, use one of the metal rings as a sliding template. When formed, fit each section individually to the blank. Glue the butt section to the blank. Slip the metal rings over the grip, and glue the forward section to the blank and to the previously mounted section.

A flared spinning-rod grip can be made of two sections, as shown in the upper two drawings, or can have a flare only at the forward end and a slip-over butt cap at the other end.

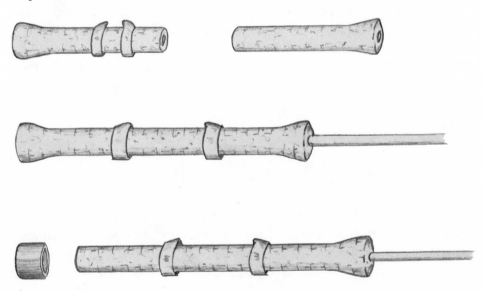

Construction steps for an all-cork handle for a very light fly rod. First the cork reel seat with flared butt end is glued on the blank, then the metal rings are put in place, and then the grip is glued on the blank.

Building this type of grip yourself is best done by turning as described above. However, if you make the grip by gluing individual cork rings to the blank and hand-sanding to shape, build only one half the grip first. Sand that half to the proper diameter and slip on the metal rings. Then build the remainder of the grip and sand it to shape. As in turning, you can use one of the metal rings as a template to get the proper diameter.

HAND-FILLING CORK GRIPS

Few rod builders will want to take the time to hand-fill the cork grips on their rods as a normal matter of course. But perhaps you are really ambitious, or are an utter perfectionist. Then again, some cold snowy evening in the middle of winter may find you restless and looking for some tedious, distracting task. In any event, you can fill the natural and inevitable pits in your cork grips.

Cork dust that occurs when cork is sanded with medium sandpaper makes the best filler. Therefore, you can save the dust from shaping operations for this purpose. The bits of cork that are removed from the inside of grips, when they are filed to fit the blank, contain a lot of "crumbs" or larger pieces and are not as good as the dust produced from sanding. You can, of course, make your dust by sanding a scrap cork ring.

You need a waterproof glue. I have had the best results with ordinary household cement (what we used to call airplane glue when I was a kid). You can also use the same cold-setting, solvent-type glue sold to bind cork to blanks. The glue should be applied only to the pits and crevices—not all over the grip. Therefore, it is best applied with a thick needle such as the flytier's dubbing needle, which comes mounted in a wood handle.

Place a drop of glue on the needle and use the needle to put the glue into the crevice in the cork. Wipe the needle with a rag. Then, with the clean needle laid on its side along the crevice, pick up any excess glue along the edges of the pit with a scraping and rolling motion. You will probably have to do this along each side of the crevice so that there is no glue outside of the pit.

Now, sprinkle more than enough dust over the glue-coated crevice than is needed to fill it. Press the dust into the pit with your finger and shake or tap off the excess. Repeat this process—I warned you that it was tedious—for each of the pits in the cork. When completed, set aside to dry overnight. Final finishing is done with very fine sandpaper.

INSTALLING RUBBER GRIPS

On some heavy-duty rods and saltwater rods you may want to use rubber composition grips. While these are preformed, the hole through the center may not fit your blank. If it slides into position snugly, you can glue it with rubber-type cement. It is very difficult to file these to fit the taper of the blank. The best method is to use a grip where the center hole is smaller than the rod blank and use the natural compressibility of this material to hold the grip firmly on the blank without glue.

Obviously, for this to work you need a very tight fit, making it difficult to get the grip into position.

First place a few layers of removable tape, such as masking tape or adhesive tape, around the bottom of the blank where you want the grip to be placed. This tape will act as a stop when you ram the grip onto the blank. Next, work up a slippery lather of soap suds or detergent and water. Using a brush, apply this liberally to the inside of the grip and the section of the blank where the grip has to slide to get to its final position against the tape. Holding the grip and blank vertically, brace the butt end of the blank against a firm support such as a workbench. Grasp the grip with both hands, and using a karate-like thrust—accompanied by a loud "Hyyah!"—ram the grip down the blank until it stops against the tape. All that remains to be done is to remove the tape, wash off the soap suds and dry with a towel.

INSTALLING WOOD RINGS AND OTHER GRIP AND HANDLE TRIM

The design you have created for your grip or handle may have included rings of wood, plastic, or other materials for trim. Sometimes you will find these listed in catalogs, but you can easily make them yourself. Secure a small piece of material, such as walnut in the thickness that matches the length of rings desired. For example, if you want to have rings ½ inch long, you will need material ½ inch thick. Determine what the finished outside diameter of the rings will be on the grip. Using a hole saw of that diameter, or just slightly larger, cut out the rings with an electric hand drill or drill press. The finished thickness of a grip is often about 1 inch, which is a common hole-saw size. I prefer the type of saw which includes a regular drill bit in the center and simultaneously drills a hole (usually ¼-inch) in the center as it cuts out the ring. The center hole can then be redrilled with a larger bit which will match the diameter of the blank. The other type hole saw does not have a drill bit in the middle and the resulting ring will be solid. You must then accurately locate the center and drill a hole the size of the blank.

An advantage of the first-type hole saw is that the ¼-inch center hole is a common size for a drill arbor such as used in a sanding disc or

A hole saw will cut neat disks from planks. This is walnut.

buffing pad. This arbor can be used to hold your wood ring in the chuck of the drill for a quick job of truing, additional shaping, or fine finish sanding. Do this, of course, before you redrill the hole to a larger size to fit on the blank.

Using the arbor, you can mount a number of rings of the same or contrasting wood for shaping and a flush fit. Depending on the length, you may have to substitute a longer bolt to thread into the arbor.

When redrilling the center hole so that the ring will fit on the blank, you may not have a bit of exactly the right size. In this case, drill a hole slightly larger than the diameter of the blank, and fill the space with string. You do not need a tight fit of the ring onto the blank, since it will be securely glued to the adjacent surfaces of the cork grip. You could drill a smaller center hole in the ring and enlarge it by filing, but this is tough, slow work with hardwood, such as walnut or cherry—I know, I have tried it. Instead, opt for the larger hole.

As mentioned earlier, dark wood rings look even better when set off by thin rings of white or colored plastic. There is quite a variety of colors made by Rohm and Haas, and you can locate a plastics retailer in the Yellow Pages. Another source is hobby stores. You will need only a small piece from which to cut a few rings about 1 inch in diameter. Retailers save the scraps they cut from large sheets, and you can purchase these for a few cents. Try thicknesses of $\frac{1}{8}$ or $\frac{1}{4}$ inch and cut them out with a hole saw the same as the wood rings. Final shaping to size can be done by placing the plastic rings on the drill arbor. A sharp cutting tool such as a wood chisel produces a clean edge. Any final finishing can be done with very fine, light-colored aluminum-oxide sandpaper.

If you want to brighten and restore the finish on any cut or shaped plastic, it can be easily done. Make a paste of a mild abrasive such as Bon Ami and water. Apply this on a piece of folded cotton cloth to the plastic while it is spun on the drill arbor. Another good mild abrasive is toothpaste. Polish with a dry cotton cloth.

In lieu of wood rings, you might want to make up a few rings of alternating colored plastics for trim, which would match the color of your guide wrappings. You may even try short lengths (about $\frac{1}{2}$ to 1 inch) of rigid plastic tubing for rings. The possibilities are endless — that is the beauty of building your own custom rod.

If you are building the grip from individual cork rings fitted and glued directly to the blank, just use your wood or plastic rings (finished to exact size as noted earlier) in place of cork rings at the position desired. If you are going to install your trim rings in a preassembled grip, make a straight cut through the grip at the point you want to place the rings, separating the grip into two pieces. Fit the butt piece of the grip, the rings, and the remaining piece to the taper of the blank in that order. When gluing in place, make certain you glue the insert rings to each other and to the ends of the cork grip sections.

Another possibility for contrasting trim in building your grip is the use of dark cork rings made of composition cork. You will rarely find these offered for sale, but you can make them by cutting slices, or rings, of any desired length from a preformed composition cork grip. As mentioned previously, this is often called "burnt cork" or "brown cork" from its color. One such grip can provide trim rings for many rods. Just be sure the outside diameter of the preformed grip is at least as great as the outside diameter of your planned grip. One advantage of dark cork for trim is that it can be located anywhere on the grip, including right under where your hand will be placed.

INSTALLING THE BUTT CAP

If your design calls for a butt cap of the slip-over variety, all you have to do is check the fit over the grip and glue into position. An excellent heavy-duty model can be fashioned from the replacement rubber caps designed to slip over metal tubular furniture legs. Readily available in hardware stores, they are sized by common tube diameters such as 3/4, 7/8, and 1 inch and will fit over grips of those outside diameters. Colors include black, white, and brown. If you find they are too long, they can be carefully cut down with an X-Acto knife or a sharp utility knife. The cut edge can be squared off by sanding, but the resiliency of rubber makes it difficult. I have had the best luck using quite coarse sandpaper backed with a wood block and shifted frequently as the paper became clogged. Finish sanding with fine sandpaper is even more difficult, since the finer grit clogs very quickly. You have to keep shifting to a new part of the paper. Caps in the same shape and sizes are also available in plastic. Not as resilient or slip-resistant as rubber, they still make fine butt caps. You can get these in a few more colors and they are less expensive. If you shorten plastic caps, cut them with a thin fine-tooth saw such as an X-Acto saw. Sanding is definitely easier; finish with the finest grade of sandpaper you can locate.

You may prefer a rubber or plastic butt cap that is fitted flush with the surface of your grip, instead of slipping over the outside. As mentioned in Chapter 5, the outside diameter of the butt cap will have to then be the same as the outside diameter of your grip. You reduce the diameter of those corks over which the butt cap will be glued. If you are shaping your grip by turning on a lathe or drill, it is an easy matter to sand down the cork at the end of the grip to match the inside diameter of the butt cap. This is one place you want a square shoulder so the joint is flush. Just hold the sandpaper steady in one place. An emery board or a strip of sandpaper glued to a popsicle stick does a good job of making the square shoulder.

If you are making your grip by gluing individual cork rings onto the blank, you will need to first reduce the outside diameter of those corks over which the butt cap will fit. An electric drill and an arbor (as

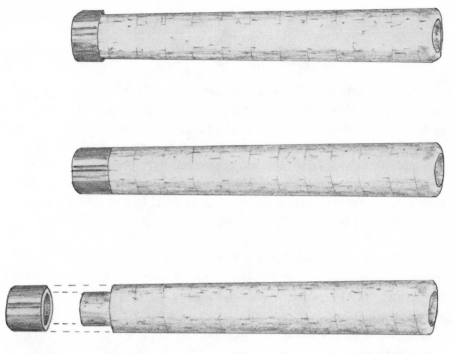

A slip-over butt cap, shown at top, is easiest to install. A flush-mounted butt cap will require turning down the cork at the butt.

discussed above in reference to wood rings) will make fast work of this sanding, but it can also be done by hand. After you have the correct outside diameter, fit the inside hole of the cork to the end of the blank. When you glue the cork in place on the blank, also glue the butt cap over the end rings. As you shape the grip it is then easy to make a flush fit between butt cap and grip.

To mount a butt cap flush on a preassembled grip, you have either to reduce the outside diameter of the end of the grip by hand sanding, or to add on a cork ring or two to accommodate the butt cap. If you go the latter route, cut off a bit of the end of the preassembled grip square so that you have a straight side of cork on which to glue the additional cork rings.

Instead of a butt cap, your design may call for a butt plate glued or screwed onto the end of the grip. This consists of a flat or convex disk made of metal or plastic. Using a hole saw, you can easily make one yourself from a plastic sheet of the desired thickness.

If you are going to mount the butt plate with a screw, countersink the center hole to accommodate a flathead screw. Fit a short length of hardwood dowel (about 2 inches long) into the inside of the end of the blank. Drill a pilot hole into the center of the dowel for the screw, then glue the dowel into the blank. After the glue dries, you simply screw the butt plate into position. Incidentally, you can have the advantages of colored plastic trim on the butt and still have a resilient nonslip surface by facing the outside of the butt plate with a rubber washer. These are made in a variety of colors and sizes with and without center holes. The outside diameter of the washer can be the same size as the plastic butt plate, or a bit smaller for a stepped-down effect. Both washer and plastic can be held in place with the screw, or the washer can be glued onto the plastic with the screw head recessed inside the center hole of the washer.

The butt plate is installed with a countersunk screw screwed into a wood dowel that has been glued into the blank.

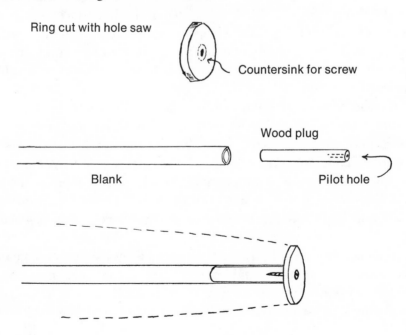

Ring cut with hole saw

Countersink for screw

Wood plug

Blank

Pilot hole

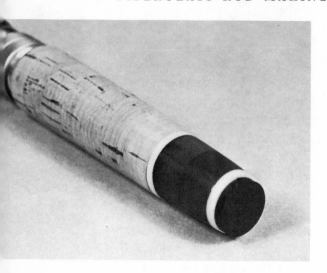

Rubber butt plate (washer) glued to hosel.

INSTALLING WINDING CHECKS AND ROD HOSELS

A simple, neat, and attractive finish can be given the front end of your handle assembly by gluing a winding check over the blank and onto the front face of the foregrip. Coat both surfaces — grip and winding check — with glue and push into place. As noted earlier, winding checks are available commercially in metal or you can make your own from a plastic disk cut with a hole saw, or even a rubber washer.

Another way of trimming the front of the foregrip is by the use of a commercial rod hosel. Here you want to blend the taper of the foregrip into the taper of the hosel. To get a smooth fit it is best to leave the outside diameter of the cork foregrip slightly larger than the widest part of the hosel. Then after the hosel is glued in place, the grip can be finish-sanded to a flush fit with the hosel. The inside diameter of the rod hosel will have to be filed to fit the blank and then glued in place.

A longer compound taper can be formed by using a combination of commercial rod hosel and matching butt cap. The butt cap is mounted over the foregrip and, of course, must have a hole drilled through the end to fit over the blank. Sand down the front of the

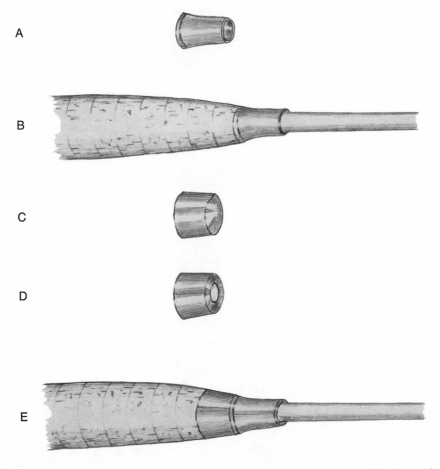

A commercial rod hosel (A) can be installed on foregrip (B). For a longer, compound taper, a matching butt cap (C) has a hole drilled in bottom (D) and is combined with a rod hosel (E).

foregrip so that the modified butt cap slips over it for a flush fit. Glue the rod hosel in place in front of the butt cap.

Rod hosels can be installed on just one end of the grip, either front or butt. They are also frequently used in matching pairs at each end, continuing the taper of the grip, and providing a symmetrical, finished appearance. Making your own hosels is easy and fun, and adds greatly to the custom look of the rod.

The two principal materials you will use are wood and plastic.

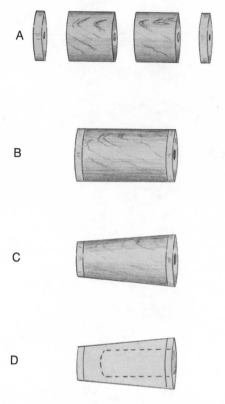

Making a butt cap or hosel. Two 1/2-inch wood rings and two 1/8-inch plastic rings (A) are glued together (B) and shaped by turning on an arbor (C). A hole the size of the blank is drilled three-quarters through to complete the butt hosel (D).

They can be used alone or combined for contrast as in wood rings. The basic construction unit is, again, the familiar ring cut out of a sheet with a hole saw.

For example, let us suppose that you want to make a walnut hosel 1 inch long with a ⅛-inch piece of white or colored plastic trim at each end. Take two ½-inch walnut rings and glue together with waterproof cement such as epoxy. If the two rings are cut from a position next to each other along the grain of a board, they can be matched for grain figure when they are glued together. Also glue a ⅛-inch plastic ring on each end (A and B). When the bond has cured thoroughly, mount this

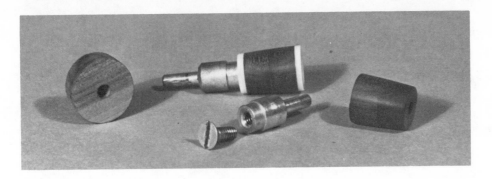

A drill arbor is used to mount rings for shaping and finishing.

assembled unit on a drill arbor, using a bolt adequate in length (about 1½ inches long). This is then chucked into an electric drill. The drill will have to be mounted in a stand or in a vise so that it will not move.

To shape the hosel into the desired taper (C), you can use any number of cutting tools such as a sharp wood chisel or wood file. A cutting tool requires a tool rest, which can be any convenient object that will raise the cutting edge to the height of the hosel in the drill. I generally use one or two pieces of scrap lumber on which I rest the chisel and feed it into the wood and plastic.

In essence, what you have just fashioned is a homemade lathe. Keep your tool rest fairly close (about ½ inch away) to the stock to be cut. This will avoid having the tool caught as the drill rotates down-

Shaping is done by scraping rather than cutting. Scrap lumber makes a firm tool rest.

All the components of a spinning-rod handle, ready for mounting on blank.

ward toward you. Feed the cutting edge slowly with your left hand, which also grips the tool rest. Your right hand should hold the handle. Remove material slowly by a scraping technique.

When the desired shape has been achieved, remove your improvised tool rest, and finish with medium, then fine sandpaper. Remove your completed hosel from the drill and the arbor. All that remains is to redrill the hole to the required size for installation on the blank. If the hosel is to be used on the butt end of the rod, do not redrill through the entire length, just about three-quarters of the way through (D). A hosel for the front end of the grip, of course, requires a hole completely through its length. The size of the redrilled hole should correspond to the diameter of the blank over which it will be installed. If you want a nonskid, shock-absorbing surface at the bottom of the butt-end hosel, glue on a rubber washer or a disk cut from a sheet of rubber. This usually looks best if the rubber is of a smaller diameter than the end of the hosel.

Using this technique you can create a great variety of hosels. You can combine wood and plastic rings in all sorts of combinations. For example: ¼-inch walnut, ⅛-inch white plastic, ½-inch walnut, ⅛-inch white plastic, and ¼-inch walnut will result in a walnut hosel with white "inlays." Alternate ¼-inch rings of walnut and white wood (poplar) will give you a "zebra" effect. It is all up to you and what you want to create.

Finishing any wood trim such as rings or hosels can be done quite simply with boiled linseed oil. Just apply with the tip of your index finger and rub it in a bit. Wipe off any excess with a cloth. This imparts a rich, dark finish to walnut and cherry and gives white wood a soft color closely approximating cork. Periodic refinishing when needed is a snap. If you prefer varnish, use one of the newer polyurethane types.

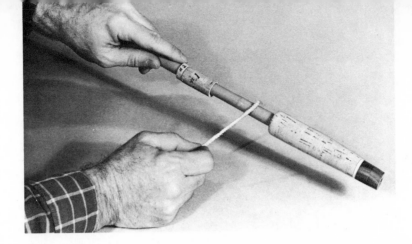

Hosel and rear grip have been glued to blank. Bushings, numbered when fitted, are slipped over blank in order as glue is applied.

Bushing that will receive bottom section of reel seat is coated with glue.

Bottom of reel seat in place. Remember to get it aligned properly with the blank.

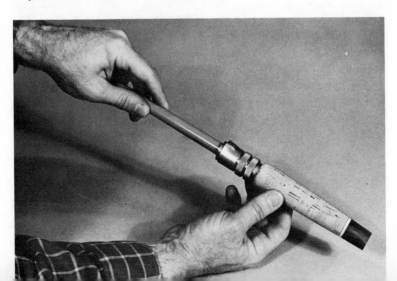

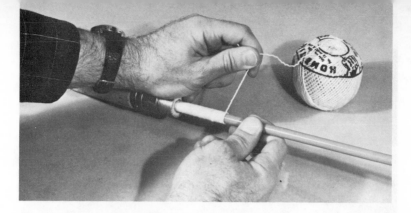

String is used to fill space for wood insert.

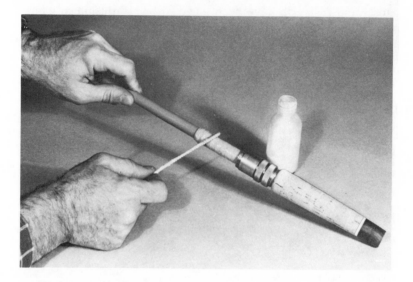

Saturate the string with glue.

Slide the wood insert over the string.

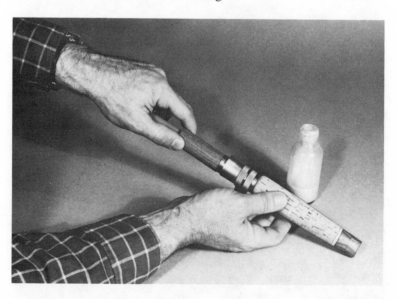

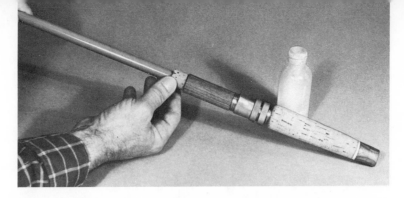

Bushing that will receive the top section of reel seat is glued in place.

The top section of reel seat is glued in place.

The first section of the foregrip is glued in place.

Trim ring is glued over string to blank.

Glue being applied for last section of foregrip.

The last section is added and the handle is complete.

7. Wrapping Guides and Trim

The proper location of guides will greatly determine how well your completed rod casts. This is definitely an area where the custom rod can be made to outperform the production model. Richness in appearance is obvious in a carefully wrapped rod. The choice of colors and styles, plain or fancy, is entirely yours; you can inject your personality into the finished rod.

LOCATION OF GUIDES

Before getting into the actual placement of the guides, there is some preparation that may need to be done. Depending upon who manufactured your blank, there may be a company name and model number printed on the blank. If you wish to remove this, it can generally be done with a rag dipped in alcohol. It may take some brisk rubbing, but in most cases the imprint will come off. On some blanks the imprint is under the final finish coat and cannot be removed. If you find it objectionable, plan a decorative butt wrap over it.

Next, carefully inspect both the top and bottom of the feet on each guide. They should be silky-smooth with no rough spots or edges, and should taper to a thin edge at the ends. Without realizing it, you can apply a great amount of pressure to a guide foot when it is wrapped into position on the rod. Any rough spots on the bottom can, in time, bite into the outer layers of fiberglass and weaken the rod at that point. Later when playing a heavy fish or tugging on a snag, the rod will break mysteriously at that point. The top of the guide foot is, of course, covered by the thread used in wrapping. Any sharp edges or rough spots here can, in a short period of time, cut the thread. So check each foot of each guide carefully. Just to be safe, I always dress top and bottom of each foot with either fine emery cloth or fine sandpaper. If you locate a bad rough spot, smooth it with a fine-tooth file and then finish dressing it with the emery cloth or sandpaper.

The last bit of preparation before locating the guides is to check the alignment of the rod to determine on which side of the blank the guides will be positioned. As discussed in Chapter 6 under "Aligning the Blank," the guides should be placed on the opposite side of the bend. You should have aligned the rod earlier and marked the male and female ferrules so that they can now be joined in exactly the right position. If you have not, please refer back to Chapter 6 now and align the rod and mark the ferrules. If you have installed a fixed reel seat on your rod, it will, of course, dictate the position of the guides on the butt section of the blank. Proper alignment should have been made before the reel seat was glued in place. If not, all is not lost. You can still align the position of the tip section relative to the butt section. Now that you know on which side of the blank the guides will be positioned, you can proceed to determine their location along the blank.

Tables of suggested guide locations are on pages 128–9. All measurements are from the tip of the rod down toward the butt. The figures given indicate the measurement at the ring of the guide. Similar tables are sometimes provided by thoughtful dealers for their specific blanks. It is best if you treat these and all such charts as only starting points, since no two rods bend exactly alike. If you have altered the action of your blank by locating the ferrule at other than the midpoint, you may have to make adjustments in the spacing even before you temporarily tape the guides in place. Similarly, you may have changed the length of your blank, or be making a rod of a length not shown on the charts. In these situations you can develop your own spacing chart by using those given as a basis for interpolation. If you find it necessary to draw up your own spacing, the following points should be kept in mind.

On *fly rods* the stripping or butt guide should be placed far enough away from the grip so that you can comfortably strip line with your left

All measurements are from tip down.
Figures are measurement in inches at guide rings.

Fly Rods

Guide #	7' 1 stripping 6 snake	8' 1 stripping 8 snake	9' 1 stripping 8 foulproof	9' 2 stripping 8 snake	3-piece 9' 1 stripping 11 snake
—	Tip	Tip	Tip	Tip	Tip
1	4	4	4	4	4
2	8	8	9	8	7
3	14	14	15	13	$10^3/_4$
4	$21^1/_2$	21	22	19	15
5	30	29	30	25	20
6	$39^1/_2$	37	39	32	$25^3/_4$
7	54	$45^1/_2$	49	44	$32^1/_4$
8	—	54	61	52	$40^3/_4$
9	—	65	75	64	$49^1/_4$
10	—	—	—	76	$57^3/_4$
11	—	—	—	—	$66^1/_4$
12	—	—	—	—	$75^1/_4$

Spinning Rods

Guide #	$5^1/_2$' 4 guides	6' 5 guides	7' 6 guides	8' 6 guides
—	Tip	Tip	Tip	Tip
1	$5^1/_2$	$4^1/_2$	4	4
2	16	11	10	12
3	28	20	18	22
4	$40^1/_2$	30	$27^1/_2$	33
5	—	41	38	$45^1/_2$
6	—	—	52	61

Casting and Spin-Casting Rods

Guide #	5½' 5 guides Tip	6½' 6 guides Tip	8' 6 guides Tip
1	4	4	5
2	10	9	12½
3	17	17	23
4	26	26	34
5	38	35½	46
6	–	46	59

hand (assuming you are right-handed) without pulling at a sharp angle. Pulling line around a corner all day puts unnecessary wear on both you and your fly line. Depending upon the length of your blank, the stripping guide should be 28 to 34 inches from the base of the butt of the rod (not the top of the foregrip). The space between guides should be progressively shorter as you move up the rod to the tip. The #1 guide (just below the top) should not be more than 4–5 inches from the tip.

On *spinning rods* the final spacing will have to be determined with the rod bent (as will be explained) and tested by actual casting with the guides taped in position. However, for starting points, the butt guide should generally be 31–35 inches from the base of the butt. The exception would be short, ultralight rods, on which it logically has to be placed closer. The butt guide must have enough distance from the fixed reel spool to allow the line to unfurl properly. This same guide must also sit high enough to prevent the line from slapping against the blank. If it is placed too close to the reel (or if the ring diameter is too small), the butt guide will choke the unfurling line too soon, reducing casting distance and placing unnecessary wear on the line. Collectively, the guides funnel the line to the tip and keep it away from the blank. The #1 guide, just below the tip, should not be farther than 5½ inches from the tip.

Having determined your tentative spacing, you are ready to measure and tape the guides to the blank. Many people suggest gluing the tip-top in position first, but I have found it easier to leave it until last. To measure, you will need a long flat space such as a workbench or table. For years I have used the family ping-pong table. First, check your fixed reel seat or the marks previously made on the ferrules for proper alignment of the rod and the side of the blank on which to place the guides. Lay the blank on the table with that side facing directly up. To prevent it from rolling, tape it to the tabletop at the grip. You will now be able to tape each guide squarely on top of the blank and have them in alignment on the correct side. When I tape the rod to the table, I position it so that the tip is flush with one end. Then it is an easy matter to hook the end of the tape measure over that end of the table and lay the tape right next to the blank. Even though I leave the tape measure in place while I attach the guides, I first mark the position of each guide with a soft lead pencil or grease pencil. Using transparent tape, attach each guide to the rod with a short piece of tape wound over each foot. Periodically, check to see that all the guides are being set in a straight line.

When all the guides are fastened in place, untape the rod from the table and sight along the guides to check their alignment. Next, cement the tip-top in position. If you are using a stick thermoplastic cement, hold it over a flame for a few seconds until it melts and daub it onto the tip. You can spread the cement with a heated knife blade or with an electric soldering gun. Quickly slip the tube of the tip-top in place and align it with the guides. The cement sets very quickly, so if your tip-top is out of alignment, just reheat the tube briefly with the soldering gun or a flame and adjust its position. When the cement has set, carefully trim away any excess cement that was squeezed out from under the tube with a razor blade.

The placement of guides is not as critical with fly rods and casting rods as it is with spinning rods. So at this point you may want to just attach reel and line to your fly rod or casting rod and go outside and cast with it for a few minutes as a final check before wrapping the guides in place. However, if you want to be really sure the spacing is correct for your rod, follow the next step outlined below for spinning rods.

The placement of guides on spinning rods requires another step.

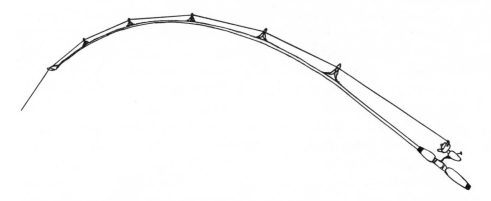

To determine proper guide spacing, position rod with
guides up in a workable arc.

Attach the reel that you intend to use with the rod and run the line
through the guides. You now want to place the rod in a workable arc
to see if the line touches the blank when the rod is flexed. This can be
done in a number of ways. If you can enlist the help of someone else,
tie the end of the line to some immovable object. Have your helper
hold the rod with the guides on *top* of the blank (upside down from
normal) and pull up on the rod until it flexes into a workable arc. If you
are working alone, anchor the butt of the rod at about a 45-degree
angle with the guides on *top*. You can do this without too much difficulty by putting the butt into a partly open drawer and then closing
the drawer against the butt. To prevent denting the cork on the edge of
the drawer front, wrap or pad the grip with a folded cloth first. To get
the rod into an arc, suspend a fairly heavy weight on the end of the
line. Or, tie down the line and turn the reel until the desired arc is
reached, locking it in place with the anti-reverse lever on the reel.

When guides are too widely spaced, the line will touch the blank.

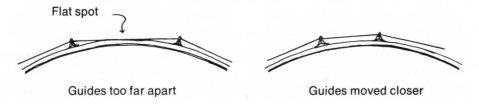

Guides too far apart   Guides moved closer

Now that you have the rod bent, check along the line to see if there are any flat spots. These are points at which the line is touching the rod. If the guides are in the proper place the line will run straight from each guide to the next guide, but it will always be held away from the blank. In all probability you will have to move two or three guides a bit along the rod. When you shorten the distance from one guide to another in order to eliminate a flat spot, you must remember that you are also lengthening the distance between the guide you moved and yet another guide—possibly creating another flat spot. For this reason it is best to work from the tip of the rod back toward the butt. Since it is usually necessary to move a few guides, I often attach the guides temporarily with "twist-ons" (paper-covered wire strips) or pieces of wire. This makes it easy to slide the guides back and forth until they are in the proper position, where they are taped.

When you have eliminated all flat spots, let the rod straighten and, once again, sight along the guides to make sure they are in line. As a final check on spacing, take the rod outside and cast with it for about fifteen minutes. See if you can detect any line slap against the blank. Check also to see if the line is cutting the tape holding your butt guide. If it is, the butt guide should be moved toward the tip by about 1/2 inch at a time. When you are satisfied that everything checks out, you are ready to wrap on the guides.

WRAPPING THE GUIDES

The home hobbyist who only wraps an occasional rod does *not* need any kind of winding device. Excellent work can be performed by hand, sitting at a desk or table. To adjust the tension of the thread, place the spool behind an open book, pull off a couple of feet of thread, and close the book. If more thread tension is needed, simply pile on additional books. Hold the rod section being wrapped at a comfortable distance in front of you. The thread will wind on easily and level if you keep the rod level. The thread coming from the book should meet the rod at a 90° angle. Try not to tip one end of the rod up or down.

If you expect to work on more than an occasional rod over the years, you may want to consider building a winding jig. There is a commercial rod-wrapping tool made for the home craftsman, but for

Winding on wraps, using a book to maintain even tension. Note the knife and tie-off loop ready to hand.

the same amount of money you can build a much better professional winding jig. The chief advantage of the commercial rod wrapper is that it takes up little space and attaches quickly to the worktable by a thumbscrew. It also does not have to be made—it is ready to go as soon as it is taken from the box. However, it is not as flexible in its use, nor does it cradle the rod nearly as well as a winding jig. It also holds only one spool of thread. Instructions for building a winding jig are found at the end of this chapter.

When winding on the thread, be careful not to use too much tension. The sizable number of turns of thread that make up a wrap can exert very heavy pressure on the guide feet. If you use tension up near the breaking point of the thread, you can damage the blank. Instead aim for just enough tension to hold the feet firmly against the blank, yet allow you to make slight guide adjustments, if necessary, when finished. You will need a piece of thread about 6 inches long for a tie-off loop. This is best made of slightly heavier thread or nylon monofilament. Also have a razor blade or X-Acto knife handy for trimming the wrap.

Just before starting the wrap, firm the transparent tape around one foot of the guide to hold it accurately in place, and carefully remove the tape from the other foot. The razor blade can be used to slice through the tape right next to the foot of the guide, facilitating removal of the tape. You will, of course, be wrapping the foot that is now no longer taped to the blank. Hold the rod so the untaped foot is toward your left hand and the taped foot toward your right.

You will wind the thread from ahead of the guide, and up over the foot—from left to right. Start the first wrap a little in front (to the left) of the foot. Lay the thread over the top of the rod and down in front of you. Bring the thread up in back of the rod and over the top, and lay the free end toward the guide. Secure this end by rotating the blank toward you, laying the thread coming from the book over the free end. You will have to hold the free end against the blank between thumb and forefinger until you have two or three wraps over it, which will hold it in position (A). If the beginning edge of the wrap became crooked when you secured the loose end, use the thumbnail of your left hand to straighten it. Continue rotating the blank with the right hand and use the thumbnail of your left hand to press the wraps tightly together. If your free end at the start was very long, cut it off close to the blank after about five or six turns so that it will be completely hidden under the wrapping. You will find that the thread will fall into position nicely if you rotate the rod fairly rapidly and keep the rod level. If you turn the blank too slowly, you will have to constantly press the thread in place with your thumbnail.

Continue winding until you are five to eight turns from the finish of the wrap. At this point stop and insert the tie-off loop—about 6 inches of slightly heavier thread (B). The tie-off thread is merely bent double and laid over the blank with the two loose ends facing to the left, away from the guide. Catch the tie-off loop with your winding thread so that about 1 inch will lie along the blank toward the guide, to your right. Wrap the remaining five to eight turns over this loop. At the finish you should have a loop of tie-off thread sticking out from under

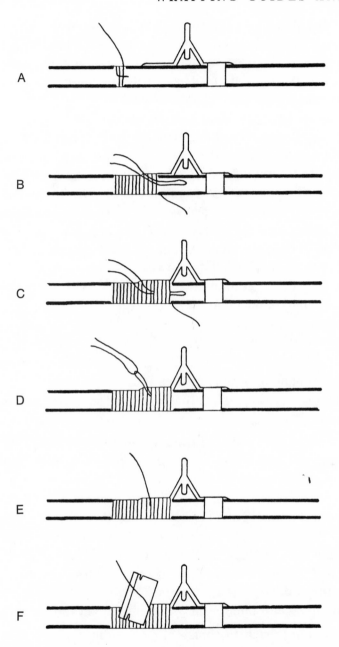

Basic winding steps. A: Wind thread over end. B: Insert tie-off loop when 5–8 turns from end. C: Wind remaining turns over tie-off loop. D: Cut thread, insert end through tie-off loop, and pull loop from under wrap. E: Pull end of thread up tight. F: Cut off thread end close to wrap with sharp blade.

135

the wrappings (C). Hold the wrap tightly between thumb and index finger of your left hand, and cut the wrapping thread about 4 inches from the rod. If you release the tension on the wrapping thread coming from the book before you cut it, you will eliminate ending up with a frayed end which is difficult to poke through the tie-off loop. Still holding the wrap in your left hand, use your right hand to insert this cut end of the wrapping thread through the loop formed by the tie-off thread (tweezers may make this easier). Now, transfer the job of holding the wrap to the right-hand thumb and index finger. Hold the wrap, but allow the free end that has been passed through the loop to dangle freely. Using the left hand, grasp *both* loose ends of the tie-off thread and pull the loop, and cut end, out from under the wrapping (D). Pull the end of the wrapping thread up tight (E). Using a sharp razor blade, trim it off as close as possible to the wrap (F).

The following suggestions may be helpful in developing and perfecting your winding technique.

1. Some people sit in a chair that has arms and use the arms to support the rod and keep it level while wrapping.

2. The amount of wrapping ahead of the guide foot may be progressively increased slightly from the smallest guides to the largest.

3. As you wrap the thread from ahead of the foot to just up over the foot, you may experience some difficulty where the windings step up on the foot. To remedy this, make sure the windings are tight together and in a straight line around the blank as you approach the foot. Take the first two or three windings farther up on the foot, purposely forming a slight space between these and the previous windings. Then, using your thumbnail, gently push these last windings to the edge of the foot (toward your left). Rotating the rod, work them into position tightly against the rest of the wrapping and pull on the wrapping thread to tighten.

4. As you approach the finish of each wrap, try to end at exactly the same place on each guide.

5. While wrapping be careful not to allow any space to remain between the threads. If they do not lie tightly together, push them into place with your thumbnail.

6. Also, watch out for any place where the thread has climbed on top of the previous turn of the thread. If you find this has occurred, unwind the thread to that point and start over.

7. Wrap all the feet to the left of each guide first. Then turn the section of the rod end for end and wrap the remaining feet, which will now once again be to your left.

In addition to wrapping the guides, you will want to wrap the ferrules and the tip-tops. Most ferrules are machined with undercuts to allow for flush thread wrappings. Start winding on the blank ahead of the ferrule and wind up over the ferrule to the end of the undercut or shoulder. Finish your wrap in the same manner as you did for the guides, using a tie-off loop. If you are using fine thread, or if the edge of the ferrule where it meets the blank is thick, you will find it difficult to step the thread up onto the ferrule. In this case you will probably have to make the wrap double thickness on the portion that covers just the blank. To do this, start your winding right at the junction of ferrule edge and blank. Wrap *away* from the ferrule. When you have covered the desired space on the blank, step the thread up on the previous windings and reverse direction, winding back over the thread to the ferrule. Continue winding right on over the edge of the ferrule and to the end of the undercut. Finish with a tie-off loop. For certain effects, or if you want to cover a ferrule which does not match the other metal fittings on the rod, the entire ferrule can be wrapped over with thread.

Tip-tops do not usually have any undercut, and the thread is wound up to the edge of the tube. Again, if you are using fine thread or the tube is thick, you may want to use a double wrap as explained

Metal ferrule wrapped with thread.

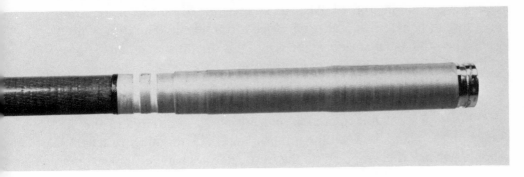

above with ferrules. Don't forget to wind on the hookkeeper just above the foregrip. It is treated the same as a regular guide except that the wrap covering the foot closest to the grip will go all the way to the grip, making it a little longer than the wrap over the other foot.

Many saltwater rods and some heavy-duty freshwater rods are wound with an underwrap on which the feet of the guide are placed. Then a second wrap of another color is made over just the guide feet in the normal manner. To do this, first mark the blank with soft lead pencil for the position of the underwrap. This will be longer than the wraps that cover the feet to allow the contrasting color of the underwrap to show at each end. The underwrap will also show through at the middle of the guide between the feet. Start your underwrap at one pencil mark, continue with one solid wrapping to the other pencil mark, and finish with a tie-off loop. Now, center the guide on top of the underwrap and tape one foot in position. Proceed to wrap the feet of the guide with the contrasting color the same as you would wrap any guide. This technique provides a nonslip, cushioned surface on which the guides rest and automatically provides contrasting color trim to the wrap. The top wrap will lie into position best if it is of slightly heavier thread than the bottom wrap. A good combination is Size A for the underwrap and Size C or E for the overwrap.

Most rods will have their appearance enhanced by the addition of a small amount of contrasting color trim at the outside edge of each wrap. For balance, confine these trim wraps to five to ten turns. The narrower trim generally looks best. A neat job can be done by starting the trim wrap against the main wrap and winding away from it. Position the rod so the completed guide wrap is to your left, and wind from left to right. Since you are making a very short wrap, you must insert the tie-off loop at the start, or immediately after you have caught the end of the wrapping thread. Also, as soon as the loose end of the wrapping thread is held fast, cut it off close to the blank. The trim wrap is performed the same as any other wrap, but due to the confined space you need to plan ahead and work carefully.

To further customize your rod and give it a more finished appearance, consider including a purely decorative wrap on the butt of the rod. For a neat, simple approach, place it about two-thirds of the distance up the blank between the foregrip and the butt guide. In length it should balance the wrapping on the butt guide—whatever looks appro-

Making an underwrap. A: Tape guide in position and mark length of underwrap. B: Make a continuous underwrap between marks. C: Tape guide in position on underwrap. D: Make guide wrap slightly shorter to allow contrasting color of underwrap to provide trim at ends.

priate to you. In design it might be the same as your other wraps: solid main color over its entire length with contrasting narrow trim wraps at each end. This is a favorite of mine, and I include an additional narrow trim wrap of black on each end. I add the extra black trim to the bottom wrap of the butt guide and to the top wrap of the hookkeeper as well. To me, this seems to help balance the extra bulk of the butt section of the rod. There are many ways to vary this decorative touch—make the decorative wrap of wide bands of your main and trim color, for example.

These, then, are the basic wraps which will give a rich, handsome appearance to any rod. Many of the most expensive production rods are finished conservatively, using just these wraps. More fancy wraps can also be used as part of the guide wraps, or as trim on the butt section of the rod. It is largely a matter of personal taste. Some rod builders simply enjoy making fancy wraps. Others feel such wraps give the rod a more custom look and make it unique. Professional custom builders find that fancy, unusual wraps help sell their rods. You will, of course, have to decide for yourself. To assist you, some of the more intricate wraps will be discussed.

OPEN SPIRAL WRAP

This wrap, as the name suggests, consists of a portion of the wrap—*not* covering the guide feet—which is open except for the single wrapping thread which spirals widely between two normal, tightly wrapped sections. It extends farther along the rod in front of the guide feet. The wrap can be made in two ways: as one continuous winding, or in two parts.

If done as one continuous winding, you must plan what length the total wrap will cover. A little more tension than normal may help. Start the wrap at the appropriate greater distance in front of the guide foot, in the normal manner, with about five turns of thread packed tightly together. Then, start the open spiral by spacing each turn the same distance from the previous turn. Just before you get to the guide foot, bring the turns of thread, once again, tightly together and complete the wrap up over the foot in the basic manner.

To perform the wrap in two parts, make a normal, basic wrap, but start it as close to the guide foot as practical. Go up, over the foot, and finish the wrap as usual with a tie-off loop. Now, turn the rod section end for end, since you will be winding in the opposite direction. Start your wrap tightly against the one you just completed and wind away from the guide for about five to six turns, keeping the thread tightly together and using a little more thread tension than usual. After the five to six turns, space your windings farther apart to form the open spiral. When you have covered the desired length with the open spiral, again bring the wrapping thread tightly together and insert a tie-off loop. Make about five to six tightly packed winds and finish.

Since the open spiral wrap is more fragile, give it an extra coat or two of varnish, epoxy, or fiberglass resin when finishing the wraps.

The open spiral wrap allows a portion of the blank to show through for contrast. For this reason, there have been many variations, or adaptations, which will place a third color underneath the open spiral wrap. This third color is different from that of the blank and from the thread used in the open spiral wrap.

A very simple way to place another color under the spiral is to paint it on the blank. Only that portion of the blank which will be seen through the spiral is painted a contrasting or harmonizing color. The proper type of paint must be chosen or it may be "lifted" by the color preserver. Most paints put up in small bottles for painting plastic models will work fine. If in doubt, give the paint a thin coat of clear (white) shellac after it has dried completely.

Another way of putting color under an open spiral is with Mylar, a very thin, but extremely tough, space-age material. This is made in gold, silver, and various metallic colors. It is available as tape with an adhesive backing and in sheets. The tape is the simplest to install. Just spiral it around the blank and trim the ends square with a razor blade. When winding the thread over the tape, you might try laying the winds of the thread in the spiral formed by the edges of the tape. If you use

Open spiral wrap over Mylar.

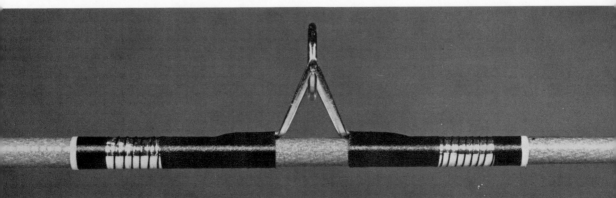

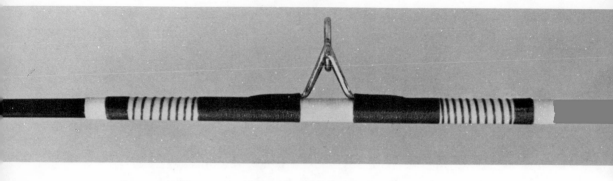

Open spiral wrap over thread underwrap.

Banded spiral wrap. After underwrap of desired length is wound, guide is centered and one foot is taped. Overwrap is made of bands of closely packed thread separated by single, open spirals.

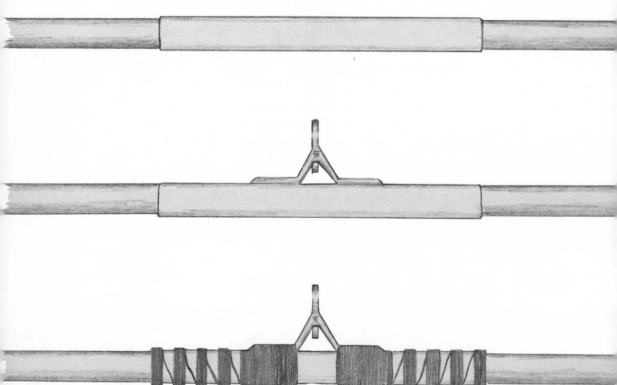

the sheet form, cut a piece just slightly wider than needed to wrap around the diameter of the blank. Taper the width slightly, to offset the taper of the blank, and fasten it so that the seam is a straight line along the underside of the rod.

The above techniques of using paint and Mylar are best when used on very light rods. On heavier rods, the preferred method of placing color under the open spiral is by using an underwrap of thread. The underwrap is installed as discussed previously, and should be of slightly thinner thread. It should extend beyond the end of the spiral overwrap. This eliminates bulk at the end of the wraps, and automatically provides a narrow band of trim color at the ends.

BANDED SPIRAL WRAP

This wrap can be used directly over the blank, or over another color. As in the open spiral wrap, the other color can be provided by paint, Mylar, or an underwrap of thread.

The banded spiral wrap is a series of narrow bands of tightly packed thread separated by open spaces. The bands are connected by a single open spiral of thread that bridges the open spaces. This allows one continuous wrapping of thread.

When used on the ends of guide wraps, you can either start the appropriate farther distance from the guide foot, and make one continuous wrap, or make the wrap in two sections as explained under the open spiral. The thread is first wound tightly together for five turns, then one open spiral turn is made. The thread is then brought back together again for five more tightly packed turns, and the single open spiral is repeated. This procedure is repeated as many times as desired, ending in a tight band under which a tie-off loop has been installed. To look professional, the open spaces should all be exactly the same size. This can be checked, as you work, by placing two pencil marks on a small card, or piece of paper. The marks should be separated by the desired length of the open space. The paper is then held against the single spiral to gauge the distance. The open spiral over each space should start on the same side of the rod, keeping the entire wrap symmetrical and balanced. The banded open spiral is particularly effective as an overwrap, especially on the butt section just above the grip.

A simple variation of this wrap is to make fairly wide bands of

White paint is applied to rod where trim bands are to appear.

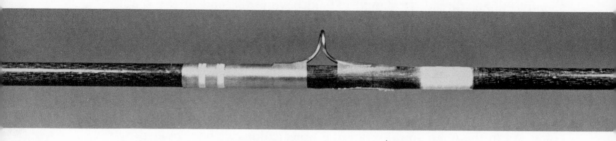

Colored Size A thread has been wound over one foot so that two white bands of paint are bridged by single spirals.

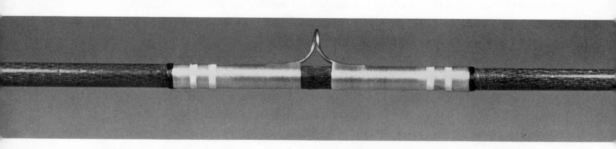

The completed wrap, with contrasting trim bands of thread at the ends.

tightly packed thread separated by narrow open spaces where the thread spirals to the next wide band. The effect achieved is one of narrow bands of the color under the wrap standing out as accents.

This technique of bridging a small open space with a single spiral of thread has as many variations as your imagination permits. The bands can consist of only three turns, or be quite wide. Narrow and wide bands can be combined in one continuous wrap, forming any combination you find pleasing. The technique is easily mastered, and you will find many applications.

DECORATIVE WRAPS
See pages 145-151 for wrapping instructions.

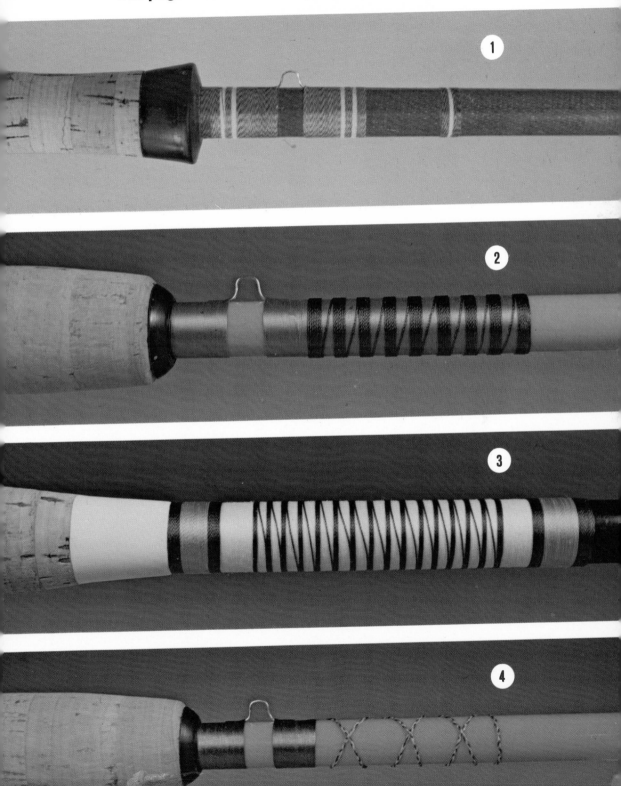

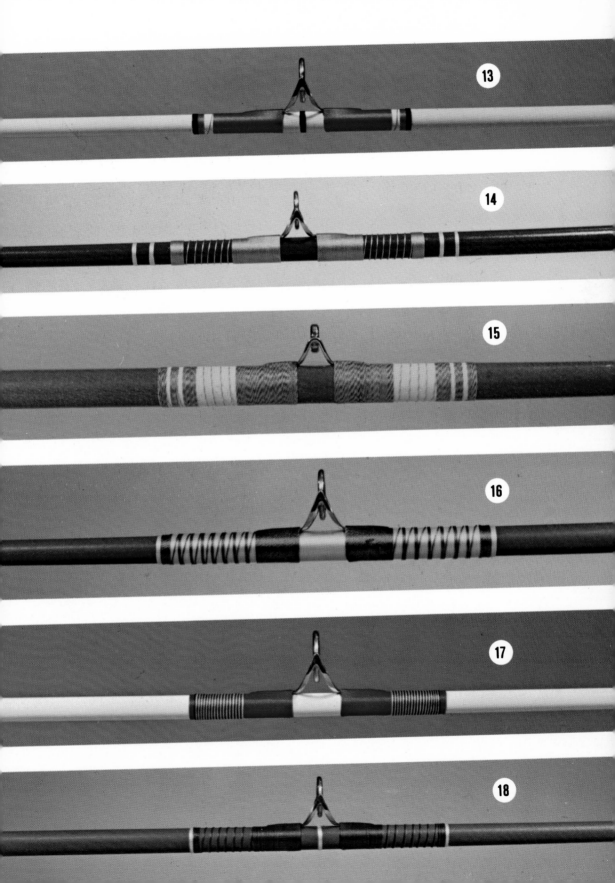

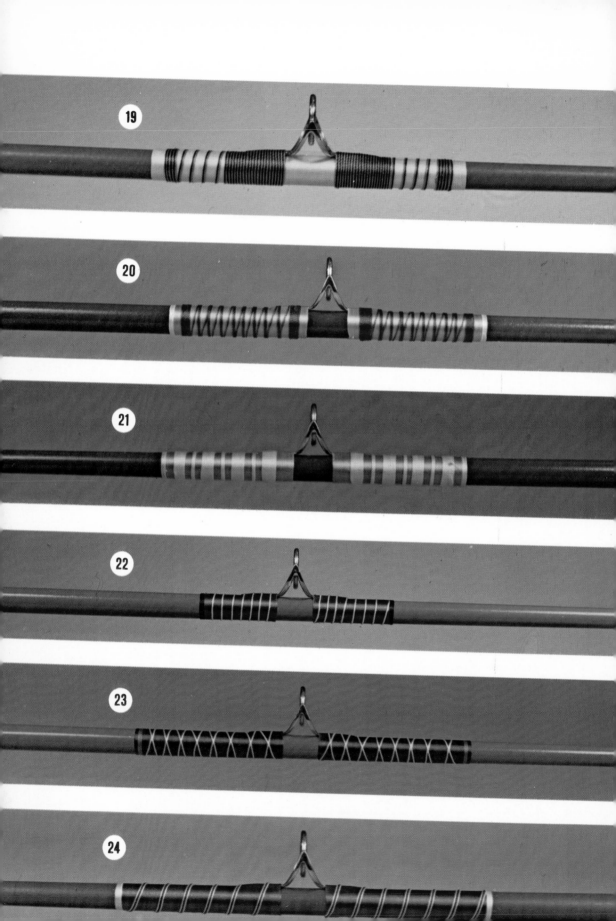

INSTRUCTIONS FOR WRAPS ILLUSTRATED IN COLOR

1. *Paint:* The yellow was first painted on the blank. When dry, the variegated thread was wound over top. The narrow bands of yellow were each bridged by a single spiral of thread. The narrow trim band farther forward was made in the same manner.

2. *Banded spiral:* The foot of the hookkeeper next to the foregrip was wound with tan Size A thread. The other foot was wound in tan, but the wrap was extended to provide a long underwrap for the remainder of the design. Size E dark-blue thread was wound over the tan. Each band of dark blue consists of the same number of winds of thread. These bands are each connected by a single spiral of thread, thus allowing one continuous winding of dark blue.

3. *Narrow banded spiral:* A long underwrap of white thread was first made. Just next to the foregrip a narrow trim band of dark-blue overwrap was made. Against this a wider band of light blue and then a narrow trim band of dark blue was made. At the other end of the white underwrap, a matching wrap of dark and light blue was added. The remaining long space of white in the middle was overwrapped with a narrow banded spiral of dark blue. This is one continuous winding in which each narrow band consists of only three winds of thread connected by an open spiral.

4. *Braid:* The braid used in this wrap was homemade of three lengths of Size E thread. The colors used were dark blue, light blue, and yellow. First, the foot of the hookkeeper away from the foregrip was taped in position and the other hookkeeper foot (next to the foregrip) was wrapped in place with green

Size A thread. One end of the braid was then taped to the blank next to the unwrapped hookkeeper foot. The braid was spiraled up and back down the rod, and the remaining end was taped. A piece of masking tape was next placed over the braid just above the point where the base wrap would be located. The two pieces of tape holding the ends of the braid were removed, and the base wrap was wound over the braid ends and the hookkeeper foot.

5. *Soutache:* The red braid used in this wrap is soutache braid, made for sewing. One end was first taped to the blank just above the foregrip. The braid was then spiraled up and back down the blank, and the other end was taped to the blank. A piece of masking tape was then laid over the braid just above (toward the tip) where the base wrap of red thread would be placed. The first two pieces of tape holding the ends of braid were then removed. The red base wrap was started next to the masking tape and wound tightly over the exposed ends of the braid. When about two-thirds of the base wrap was completed, the ends of the braid were cut with a razor blade. The base wrap was finished with a tie-off loop against the foregrip. A narrow white overwrap was added for trim just above the foregrip.

6. *Butt Wind:* This is commercial braid sold under the name "Butt Wind." First, a long underwrap of white thread was made. One end of the braid was taped in place just above the foregrip and the braid spiraled up and back down the rod, over the white underwrap. The other end was then taped in place. A piece of masking tape was laid over the braid just above where the blue base wrap was to be located. The two pieces of tape holding the ends of the braid were removed, and the light-blue base wrap wound over the ends of the braid. Two narrow trim bands of dark blue were wound over the light-blue base wrap, one at each end. A similar wrap of light and dark blue was added above the end of the spiraled braid (toward the tip).

7. *Two-thread overwrap:* The extended hookkeeper wrap of light-blue Size A thread becomes the underwrap for this design. Starting next to the foregrip a very narrow trim band of black was wound over the light blue. Next, a wider band made of two threads—black and white in Size E—was made. The two threads were wound at the same time and handled as if they were one thread. Another very narrow trim band of black was added. On the other side of the hookkeeper, the same two-thread overwrap was repeated. Next, a white overwrap was made. The spaces where the blue underwrap shows through were each bridged with a single spiral of white thread. Finally, the two-thread overwrap was repeated once more.

8. *Overwrap:* The blank was first covered with an underwrap of long bands of black, yellow, and white in Size A thread. Starting at the foregrip, narrow bands of black and yellow were wound over the white. A space was skipped, to allow the white to show through, and the same pattern of black and yellow was repeated two more times. In the middle of the yellow underwrap a band of red was wound over top. This was trimmed on each end by a very narrow band of black. The remaining long white band was overwrapped with black and yellow exactly the same as near the foregrip.

9. *Diamond:* This is the diamond wrap discussed in detail in the text. Briefly, it is made of fine colored bands each four threads wide and two black bands two threads wide. The bands were spiraled up and back over a white thread underwrap, and were taped to the hosel on the foregrip. The green band was wound on first. Then on each side of the green was spiraled a band of white, followed, again on each side, by a band of red. Finally, the narrow black bands were wound one on each side of the red. The red base wrap was started away from the foregrip and wound toward it. When it was about half completed, the tapes holding the bands to the hosel were removed and the individual threads cut to length. The base wrap was then completed over the cut ends and up to the foregrip.

10. *Diamond variation:* Wound here on a heavy fly rod, the extended hookkeeper wrap of light blue forms the underwrap. The first band spiraled was the white, made of four threads. On each side of the white a four-thread band of dark blue was wound. Then, on each side of the dark blue, a white band two threads wide was added, followed by a dark-blue band also two threads wide. All bands were taped to the blank next to the foregrip until covered by a dark-blue base wrap. A band of dark-blue trim was overwrapped next to the foregrip.

11. *Chevron:* This is the chevron wrap discussed in detail in the text. Briefly, it consists of five different colored bands, each four threads wide, spiraled over a white thread underwrap. When each band was wound in position it was taped to the hosel on the foregrip. The first band wound was dark blue. Then, in the following order, each to the right of the previous band: light blue, orange, light blue, dark blue. The dark-blue base wrap was started away from the foregrip and wound toward it. When it was about half completed, the tapes holding the bands were removed and the threads cut to length. The base wrap was then completed over the cut ends and up against the foregrip.

12. *Corkscrew:* This interesting wrap consists of a black band of twelve threads spiraled over a long white wrap. At the end of the wrap toward the tip of the rod, the black threads are "tied under," or held in place underneath the white wrap. Therefore, it was essential that the wrap be started at this end and wound toward the butt.

Initially, twelve black threads, Size E, were cut to the appropriate length. These were laid parallel to the rod and taped in position, in groups of four, so that the ends would be covered and anchored by the start of the white wrap. The white thread was wound over the ends of the black thread and all the way to the foregrip. Next, one band of four black threads was untaped and untangled. Keeping the threads flat, they were spiraled over the white to the foregrip and taped. The width of the spiral was gauged so that when all twelve threads were added, the width of the black band would be approximately the same as the width of the white wrap showing through. Each of the other bands of four black threads was then wound tightly against the previous spiral and taped next to the foregrip.

A black base wrap was started a short distance away from the foregrip and wound toward it, over the black spiraled threads. When the base wrap was about half completed, the twelve black threads were untaped and cut so that their ends would be hidden under the base wrap. The base wrap was then wound the remaining distance to the foregrip and finished with a tie-off loop.

13. *Guide ring:* The narrow black guide-ring trim was wound on the blank first. Then the guide was taped in position while one foot was wrapped. Starting away from the guide, and winding toward it, a narrow band of closely packed orange thread was made. A single open spiral of thread allowed the white blank to show through, and the orange thread was again wound closely together up over the guide foot. Finally, the narrow black trim bands at each end were added.

14. *Open spiral:* The blue thread was started an appropriate distance away from the guide, and first wound in a closely packed band. It was then wound in seven open spirals to a point just in front of the guide foot. The thread was then brought back together and a solid band of blue thread was wound up over the guide foot. Two separate narrow white trim bands were added to each end of the wrap.

15. *Underpaint:* The blank was first painted yellow on each side of the guide feet. When dry, brown variegated thread was wound starting away from the guide. First a narrow band of thread was made, followed by a single open

spiral to allow the yellow to show through. This was repeated, and a slightly wider band of closely packed thread followed. Four open spirals of thread bridged the space to the final wrap over the guide foot.

16. *Narrow banded overwrap:* Before the guide was taped into position, a long wrap of white Size A thread was made. One foot of the guide was then taped on top of this underwrap. Size E green thread was started on top, and just inboard, of the end of the white. A narrow band of green was made and then a series of open spirals with very narrow bands—three threads wide—was wound up to the foot of the guide. One long band of green was continued over the foot of the guide.

17. *Two-thread overwrap:* A regular basic wrap of red Size A thread was made over each guide foot. To allow the narrow trim bands of red to appear on each end of the wrap, the two-thread overwrap was started just in from the ends and wound toward the guide. One black and one white Size E thread were wound simultaneously over the red basic wrap to a point just in front of the guide foot. When winding the two threads, they were held together and treated the same as one thread, including the finish with a single tie-off loop.

18. *Two-thread open spiral:* Before the guide was taped to the blank, the narrow white guide-ring trim wrap was made of Size A thread. Next, the guide was taped in position and two Size E threads, black and orange, were wound simultaneously as one thread. A narrow band of closely packed thread was followed by a series of seven open spirals. Just in front of the guide foot, a solid wrap was started and wound over the guide foot. The black and the orange thread were treated as one thread throughout the winding, including the finish with a single tie-off loop. The narrow white trim bands on each end were completed last.

19. *Two-thread overwrap:* A long underwrap of white Size A thread was made first. To provide the white bands at each end, the overwrap was started a short distance in from the end. Two Size E threads, one black and one orange, were wound at the same time and handled as one thread. First, a closely packed band was made. This was followed by four open spirals and then a closely packed section over the guide foot.

20. *Narrow banded overwrap:* A basic wrap of light-blue Size A thread was first made to secure the guide foot. Size E purple thread was started just inboard of the blue and wound over it. The purple overwrap was started in a band to anchor the thread. This was followed by a series of open-spiraled, very nar-

row bands, each three threads wide. These spiraled bands were continued over the previously wrapped guide foot and finished in a band just short of the end of the light-blue basic wrap. The narrow trim bands of white Size A thread were added last.

21. *Alternate bands:* A basic wrap of light-blue Size A thread was first made over each guide foot. An overwrap of white Size E thread was started a short distance from the end of the blue. Wide and very narrow bands were alternated to allow the blue to show through. Each band was connected by a single spiral of thread (on the opposite side from that seen in the photo). The white trim bands at the end were added last and were made of Size A thread.

22. *Tied-under spiral:* As you will note, the white thread which is spiraled over the brown basic wrap terminates next to the guide ring without the usual band associated with a tie-off loop. This is because the white thread is anchored underneath the brown wrap. To make this type of wrap it is necessary to start right next to the guide ring and wind the brown basic thread *away* from the guide. This is opposite from the technique used in most wrapping.

A suitable length of white Size E thread was temporarily taped in position so that its end would be covered when the brown wrap was started. Size A thread was used for the brown wrap, and it was completed with the usual tie-off loop. Next, the white thread (with its end now tied under next to the guide ring by the brown wrap) was spiraled over the brown and slightly beyond the end. The white thread was then temporarily taped in position. The narrow black trim band was started against the brown and wound over the white thread to anchor it. When the black band was almost completed, the white thread was untaped and cut close with a razor blade. A few more turns of thread were made to complete the black trim. More detailed explanations of this technique are provided in the text.

23. *Tied-under cross spiral:* The white threads forming the cross spirals are held in place underneath the blue basic wrap at the ends nearest the guide ring. At the opposite ends of the wrap, the white threads are anchored by wrapping the orange trim bands over the white threads. Therefore, since the white thread was to be "tied under" near the guide ring, the basic blue wrap was startted up on the guide foot right next to the ring, and wound away from the guide.

First, two Size E white threads of suitable length were temporarily taped in position so that the blue basic wrap would cover the ends. Dark-blue Size A thread was wound over the white ends and away from the guide ring. When the desired length of the blue wrap was reached, it was completed with a tie-off loop in the normal manner. Next, one of the white threads was un-taped and spiraled over top of the blue basic wrap to a point just beyond the end of the blue. There it was taped to the blank. The other white thread was then untaped and spiraled in the opposite direction so as to form the crosses or x's. It, too, was wound beyond the end of the blue wrap and then taped to the blank.

Orange Size A thread was then started against the end of the blue wrap and wound over top of the white thread. A couple of turns before the end of the orange band, the white threads were untaped and cut close with a razor blade. The last two turns of orange covered the cut ends. A very narrow trim band of dark blue was added next to the orange to finish the wrap.

24. *Three-thread spiral:* The three threads forming the spiral are "tied under" the brown basic wrap. Therefore, winding was started next to the guide ring and wound away from the guide. First, the three Size E threads (white, black, and white) were laid parallel to the blank and temporarily taped in position so that the brown basic wrap would cover their ends. Next the brown wrap, Size A thread, was wound over the white ends and away from the guide ring. It was finished in the usual manner with a tie-off loop.

The three Size E threads were then all untaped and spiraled together, as one thread, over the brown wrap. Care had to be taken to keep the three threads flat and always in the proper order: white, black, white. The spiral was wound a bit beyond the end of the brown wrap and then taped to the blank. White Size A thread was wound in a band, next to the end of the brown, and over the top of the three threads forming the spiral. A few turns before the end of the white band, the three spiral threads were untaped and cut close with a razor blade. The remaining turns of white covered the cut ends and completed the wrap.

INDIVIDUAL TRIM BANDS

The banded spiral wrap (pages 143–4) works when you want a series of closely spaced bands of color. However, there are times when you will want only one or two bands not connected by a spiral of thread. This can be just off the end of a guide wrap or it can be part of the decorative trim on the butt. These bands may be wound directly over the blank or over paint, Mylar, or an underwrap. They are made the same way as the narrow trim bands discussed under the basic wraps. The only difference is that they will not be placed tight against the guide wrap, but will stand alone. Start the wrap in the usual manner. As soon as the end of the thread is secured under the windings (two or three turns), insert the tie-off loop. After one more turn with the thread, cut off the loose (beginning) end of the thread. Complete the wrap with a few more turns, and finish with the tie-off loop. Before cutting off the loose end that has been pulled under, make sure you pull it up tight.

Guide-ring trim with a basic wrap. A: Wind on guide-ring trim. B: Tape one foot of guide in position. C: Make a basic wrap. D: Add trim bands at ends.

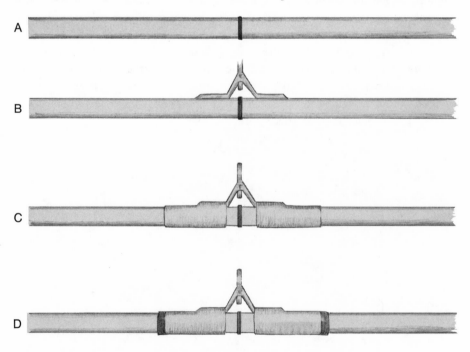

Since these trim bands are narrow, it may be necessary to straighten the edges after the wrap is completed. Do this with your thumbnail while rotating the rod.

A specific application of the individual trim band just discussed is as a narrow band of thread directly under each guide ring. It can be used in combination with any other wrap. When used with a basic wrap, it is usually the same color as the trim bands that are placed tight against each end of the guide wrap. Since it is placed under the guide, it obviously should be wrapped onto the blank before the guide is taped into position.

Split underwrap

The basic underwrap, as explained earlier, is one long wrap over which the two shorter guide wraps are placed. The underwrap shows through beneath the guide. A simple variation—the split under-wrap—is really two wraps with a space between. The space allows the blank to show through (see illustration, page 154). Both underwraps and the overwraps end at the same points nearest the guide ring.

To make this wrap, first position the guide on the blank. Mark the points on each side of the guide ring where both underwrap and overwrap will terminate. Also mark the points in front of the guide feet where the underwraps will begin. Starting at that point, make a continuous wind up to the mark where the overwrap will end near the guide ring. Skip the space where the blank will show through beneath the guide, and make the underwrap for the other guide foot.

The shorter overwraps are wound on in the normal manner. They should terminate at exactly the same spot as the underwrap.

DECORATIVE BUTT WRAPS

The butt section of the blank, above the foregrip, generally has a decorative wrap. It may be a conservative, basic wrap located somewhere between the end of the foregrip and the first guide, or it may be very fancy and occupy much of this total space. Heavy rods seem to be best suited to the longer, more complicated wraps.

Split underwrap. A: Locate ends and middle section of underwrap. B: Make separate underwraps between marks. C: Tape guide in position. D: Complete guide wrap. Note that color of blank shows through in center beneath guide.

If you would like to so decorate your rod, a little creativity will enable you to combine ideas and techniques previously discussed. All kinds of trim can be worked out using a combination of underwraps and overwraps. All that is necessary is a little planning beforehand and perhaps a sketch to follow as you work. A few ideas not mentioned before are listed below.

PREPARED FLAT TAPE

One of the easiest materials to work with is specially prepared flat tape made just for fancy butt wraps. This is not always the easiest thing to find, but there are a number of types available. One type consists of two colors of winding thread attached to a thin tape backing. Different color combinations are available. The tape can be wound onto the blank in different ways to produce varied effects. With careful work a diamond-wrap effect can be achieved.

Butt-wrapping materials. The soutache braid is available at notions counters.

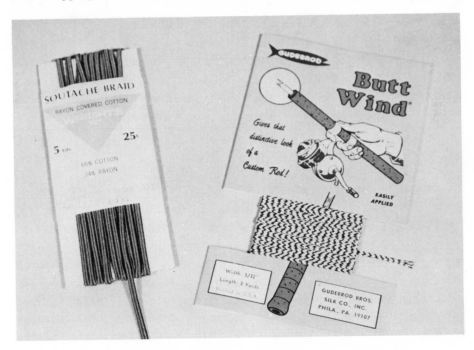

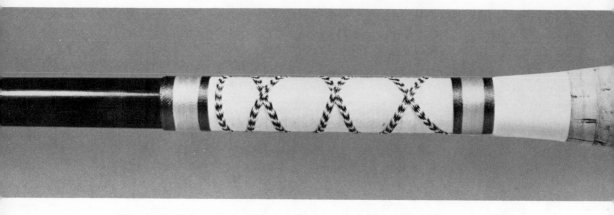

"Butt Wind" is spiraled over an underwrap and anchored by a two-color base wrap. A matching decorative wrap is placed at upper end.

Another type of tape is not faced with wrapping thread, but gives a textured, threadlike appearance. This looks well when used as a solid band trimmed at each end with one or two narrow thread wraps. It is also a good material for an underwrap. Various fancy thread overwraps and trim wraps can be placed on top. Of course, plain colored thin plastic tape and Mylar can be used in a similar fashion on the rod butt.

All tapes, regardless of how they are wound on the blank, should have their ends covered with a thread overwrap. This overwrap should extend beyond the edge of the tape. It acts not only to conceal the edge of the tape, but to prevent it from lifting in the future.

BRAID WRAP

Occasionally you can buy a braid specifically sold for butt decoration. However, any twisted or plaited braid that is not too thick or bulky can be used. The preferred shape is oval or round. You can even make your own for use on lighter rods by plaiting a number of lengths of heavy thread, such as Size E or larger. This can be one solid color, or more frequently, two or three colors. For some variety you may want to check the notions section of a department store or fabric store. Soutache braid, and other braids for use in sewing, can be put to excellent use on heavier rods as a decorative butt wrap.

156

The braid is wrapped in an open spiral up the blank, and then reversed, and spiraled back down the blank. The resulting pattern is of curved crosses or X's. To make the wrap, first determine the length needed by a loose test wrap. Use a piece a bit longer than this test indicates.

The braid must be anchored under a solid wrap of thread at the base of the butt. This is referred to as a base wrap, and is wound on after the braid is in place. The ends of the braid are temporarily held in position with tape.

To make a braid wrap, first determine the length and position of your base wrap. Mark the blank with a grease pencil or soft lead pencil. Tape one end of the braid just below this mark and spiral the braid up the rod. Take care to keep the distance between the spirals uniform. When you have covered the desired length of the rod, make a straight turn around the blank (at 90° to the axis of the rod). Now reverse the direction of your spirals and wind the braid back down the rod. Make certain that the returning spirals are spaced exactly the same as those that travel up the rod. The crosses that are formed should all appear in a straight line on each side of the rod. Use fairly heavy tension as you wind the braid.

When you have returned the spiraled braid to the starting point, tape the end to the blank. Place a piece of masking tape over the braid and around the blank just above the mark you made to indicate the position for your base wrap. This will hold the braid, under tension, while you cover the ends with the thread of the base wrap. You can now remove the two pieces of tape from the ends of the braid.

Start your base wrap at your previous pencil mark, which should now be immediately below the strip of masking tape holding the spiraled braid. Wind over the braid and toward the butt. When the base wrap is about one-half to two-thirds complete, cut the ends of the braid close with a razor blade. Continue winding over the cut ends and finish with a tie-off loop.

If you are going to include a hookkeeper between the foregrip and the braid, plan accordingly. First, wrap the foot of the hookkeeper closest to the foregrip. Leave the other foot unwrapped. The second foot will be covered by the same base wrap that secures the braid.

When ready to apply the first coat of color preserver, check to see that the braid is still wrapped tightly on the blank. If it has loosened,

The wrap that holds the forward foot of the hookkeeper also anchors the ends of the braid.

you can tighten it again by carefully pushing the braid up on the blank away from the butt. Hold it in that position by the top loop while applying color preserver. If you still have trouble with it slipping, tape the top loop to the blank and give the remainder of the braid a few coats of preserver. This will hold it fast to the blank. Remove the tape and give that section the same number of coats.

Because of the slightly greater bulk of the braid, an extra-heavy finish is required over it for protection. More than the usual number of coats of varnish, epoxy, or fiberglass resin should be used. This will help fill in around the edges of the braid and give it a smooth appearance.

DIAMOND WRAP

One of the most admired, and attractive, butt wraps is the intricate diamond wrap. This is made of bands of different color, usually four threads wide, spiraled up and down the rod in the same manner as the braid explained above. When the bands are applied in the proper sequence, a pattern of concentric diamonds of different colors will result.

An underwrap of one solid color is recommended. The friction between the two layers of thread helps hold the diamond wrap in place while it is being applied. The underwrap also provides color contrast, effectively setting off the pattern.

The four threads, making one band of color, are all wound at the same time. This is really easier than it sounds. To determine the lengths of thread, spiral a test thread up and back over the desired area of the blank. Measure the test thread. Allow a few extra inches, and cut two threads to double that length. Fold these two threads in the middle for the desired four working threads.

Suspend the two threads, by their middle, over your fingers and allow them to dangle freely. Make sure they are not twisted together. If you run the fingers of your other hand loosely through the threads, any twist will be eliminated.

The folded ends of the thread are taped flat to the tapered foregrip or hosel with strips of masking tape. If the foregrip is not tapered, tape the threads to the blank immediately above the foregrip with narrow strips of tape. Masking tape works better than cellophane tape because it is easier to remove and does not leave a sticky residue.

Now, keeping the threads flat and together, wrap on the first band. Grasp the threads close to the blank. Using plenty of tension, spiral the thread up the blank. When you have covered the desired distance on the blank, make your final turn around the rod at a 90° angle. Reverse direction and spiral the threads back down, toward the butt. Hold the end under tension while you tape it to the foregrip or blank. The position of the first band of thread is critical. If it does not lie on the rod in exactly the right position, the finished diamond wrap will be crooked and unsymmetrical. The space between each spiral should be exactly the same, and the crosses, or X's, should be all in a line on opposite sides of the rod.

I have found that the best way to accomplish this is to hold the thread at a constant angle to the rod as the thread is spiraled up the blank. When the return spiral is started, hold each cross with the index finger and thumb of the left hand while you lay the thread in position to the next cross with your right hand. Do not release your grip with the left hand until you have the second cross lined up perfectly. Repeat this process from one cross to another as you bring the thread back down the blank. After the end of the thread is taped down, carefully check the position of your first band. Sight along the rod to make sure the crosses are in a straight line on each side of the rod. You can further check alignment of the crosses by holding a straightedge along them. Minor repositioning of the threads can be done with your thumbnail. However, if the first band is off by much, untape one end and rewrap it. All other bands will follow this one, so it is worth the time and effort to get it correctly positioned.

The next two bands will each be the same color. They will be wrapped one on each side of the first. Again, tape the folded end of the threads down and wind the four threads together under heavy tension. Make sure they lie flat and tight against the first band. If, as you wrap, you feel the threads becoming twisted as they enter your wrapping hand, stop and gently straighten them with the fingers of the other hand. The last two bands of color will again be added one on each side of the wrap. Normally, only five bands are used: a single color in the middle bordered by paired bands of two other colors.

At this stage, all the wraps are in position, but are held there by tape. They must be anchored by a base wrap. Start your base wrap above the foregrip and wind toward the foregrip. Use plenty of tension, and make the base wrap fairly wide so that it will hold the threads under it tightly in place. When the base wrap has covered one-half to two-thirds of the distance to the foregrip, stop. Remove the tape and cut the threads forming the diamond pattern with a razor blade. Cut the threads so that they go almost to the foregrip. If they are too long they will stick out of the bottom end of the base wrap. Small pointed scissors may be of help here.

When the threads are all cut to the proper length, insert your tie-off loop into your base wrap. Complete the base wrap over the cut threads and up to the foregrip. Cut your winding thread and finish. Check the entire wrap carefully. It is generally necessary to firm some threads into position against each other with your thumbnail. As with all heavier wraps, give it extra coats of color preserver and final protective finish.

Using the same basic technique, quite a few variations are possible. For example, a narrow accent border can be added to the five-band pattern. Simply wind a two-thread band on each side of the existing diamond wrap. The width of any band of color can be varied by using more or less threads. If you decide on a band more than four threads wide, it is suggested you wrap it on in two steps. Otherwise, it becomes difficult to keep it flat and untwisted.

The pattern that is formed depends on the position of each band. As noted above, a series of diamonds are formed by placing bands of the same color on each side of the initial, single band. In other words, first the middle color is wound on. Then a band of the second color is wound *on each side* of the initial band—one on the left and one on the right. The third color is then added by winding two more bands, one *on each side* of the previous wrap.

Perhaps an example will help clarify this. If we wanted a diamond wrap where the center of each diamond was green, bordered by white with an outside border of red, we would wrap as follows:

> 1st band green
> 2nd band white, wound to the *left* of the green
> 3rd band white, wound to the *right* of the green
> 4th band red, wound to the *left* of the white
> 5th band red, wound to the *right* of the white

Diamond wrap sequence. The first band (green) is wound over the underwrap.

The second band (white) is wound to the left of the green.

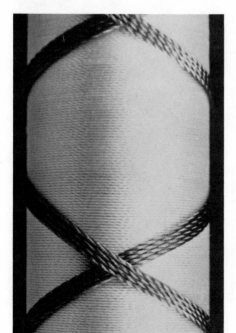 

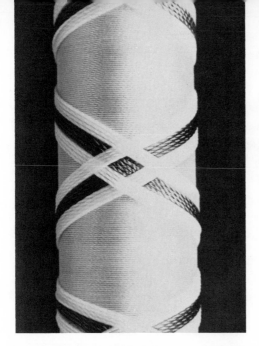

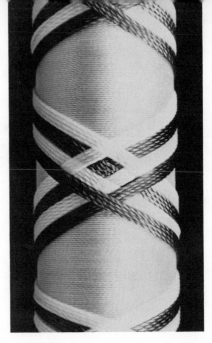

The third band (white) is wound to the right of the green.

The fourth band (red) is wound to the left of the white.

The fifth band (red) is wound to the right of the white.

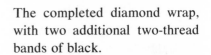

The completed diamond wrap, with two additional two-thread bands of black.

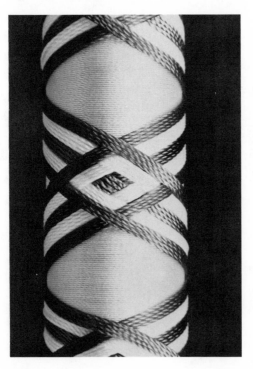

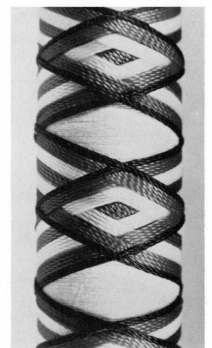

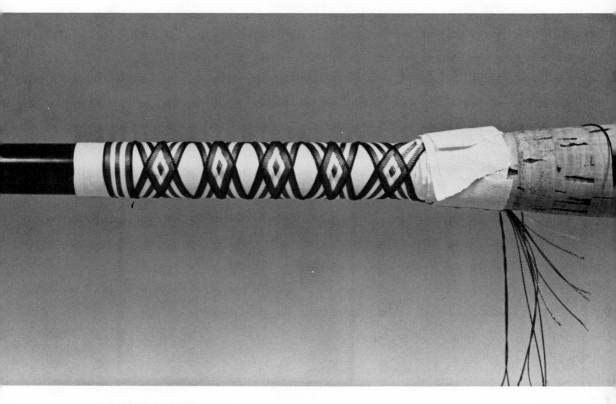

The completed diamond wrap before the base wrap has been applied to anchor the threads.

A variation that I call the chevron wrap is wound with each band wrapped *to the right* of the preceding band. Instead of a pattern of diamonds being formed where the bands cross, a pattern of chevrons results.

Again, let's look at an example. Suppose we wanted chevrons to appear in the following order:

> Dark blue
> Light blue
> Orange
> Light blue
> Dark blue

Chevron wrap, made by winding each band of color to the right of the preceding band.

We would wrap the bands in that order, always adding the next band *to the right* of the preceding band:

> 1st band dark blue
> 2nd band light blue, wound to the *right* of the dark blue
> 3rd band orange, wound to the *right* of the light blue
> 4th band light blue, wound to the *right* of the orange
> 5th band dark blue, wound to the *right* of the light blue

As with the diamond wrap, the chevron version can be varied by using bands consisting of different numbers of threads. You can also use more or less than five bands. Once mastered, these wraps present great opportunities for your creativity. Go ahead, experiment — and have fun!

Two-thread wrap

An unusual, almost iridescent effect can be achieved in wraps by simultaneously winding two threads of different colors. This technique is applicable to guide wraps or butt wraps. It can be used for the entire

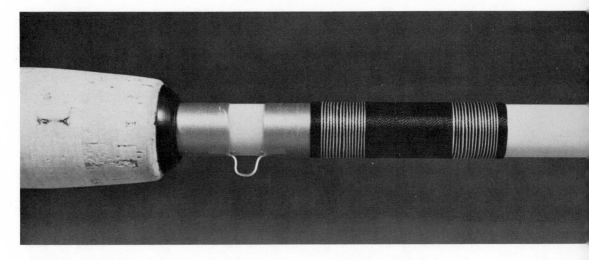

Two-thread wrap used as part of a decorative butt wrap. One black and one white thread, Size E, were wound together.

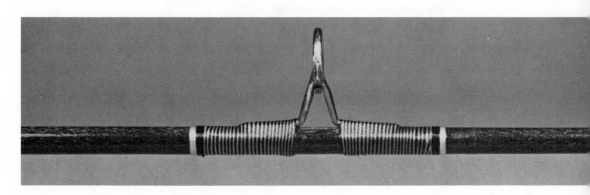

Three-thread wrap (black, orange, and white), of Size A thread. A two-thread wrap of Size E thread would have been too bulky for this very light rod, and two threads in Size A would not show up properly.

wrap or just a portion of it, over an underwrap of contrasting color or directly on the blank.

You can experiment with different color combinations to find those most pleasing to you. I have found black and white produces a "silver" effect when viewed from a normal distance. Black and orange gives a "copper" effect. If the thread is very thin, such as Size A, the effect is lost somewhat. I have had the best results using Size E.

To make a two-thread wrap you need a device to keep equal tension on both threads. If you are using a book, place the two spools together in back of the book and feed the threads side by side between the pages. If you are using the professional winding jig (explained at the end of this chapter), simply mount the two spools on the thread holder.

All winding operations are done in exactly the same manner. Just treat the two threads as if they were one thread. This can best be done if you bring the threads together about one to two inches above the blank and feed them through thumb and forefinger of your right hand. The job of revolving the rod can be done with your left hand. When starting a wrap, the two threads are looped around the blank and over the loose ends, in exactly the same manner as you would use for one thread. While winding, you must watch to see that one of the threads does not get laid on top of the previously wound thread. Each wind must lie flat, and against the preceding wind. Your right hand makes sure the threads do not become twisted.

The wrap is finished in the normal fashion. A few turns before the end a tie-off loop is inserted. At the end of the wrap, both threads are cut and their ends inserted through the tie-off loop. After these ends are pulled under the previous windings with the tie-off loop, snug them up tight and cut them off as close as possible with a razor blade. The very end of the wrap, where the two threads disappear under the windings, can be straightened by pushing across the top of it with your thumbnail.

TYING UNDER

On some guide wraps and butt wraps, the design requires that a spiraled thread, or group of threads, end flush with the end of the basic underwrap. There is no band of closely packed thread, formed from the spiraled thread, under which the end can be pulled with a tie-off loop. The spiral just appears to terminate at the end of the wrap. This effect is achieved by a technique called tying under.

Whenever you desire a wrap to end in this fashion, you must start the wrap at that point and wind away from it. This is true even if the normal winding would not terminate at that end. For example, guide wraps are normally started on the blank in front of the guide, wound

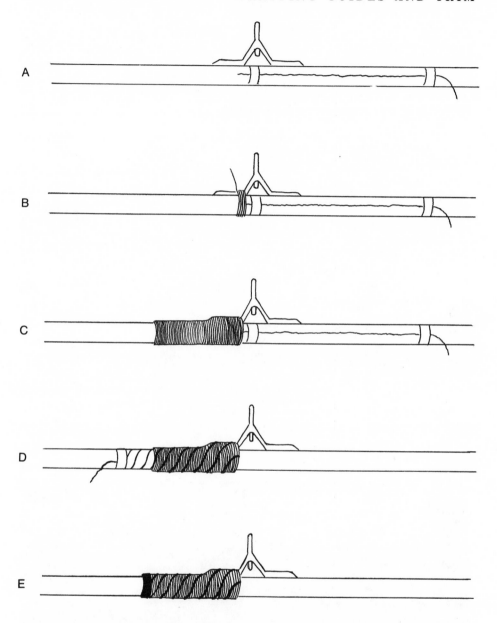

Steps in tying under. A: Tape thread for spiral to blank. B: Start underwrap over end of spiral thread. C: Complete underwrap. D: Untape spiral thread, wind it over the underwrap, and tape it to blank. E: Anchor spiral thread with trim band.

over the guide foot, and ended near the guide ring. However, if a spiral is to end flush with the underwrap just next to the guide ring, you know you must start at that point and wind away from the guide, ending on the blank in front of the guide. Therefore, your initial winds of thread would be as close as possible to the guide ring, and would surround both the blank and the guide foot.

The first step in tying under is to lay the predetermined length of thread, or group of threads that will form the spiral, parallel to the rod in a position where the ends will be covered when the basic underwrap is started. These threads will be running away from the wrap in the opposite direction that the wrap will be wound. Only a small length of their ends will be in position to be covered. When this position is achieved, temporarily tape the threads to the blank to keep them out of the way when you wind on the basic underwrap (A).

Start the basic underwrap as you would any other wrap, but wind over the ends of the thread taped in position (B). Wind the desired length, and terminate the basic underwrap as usual with a tie-off loop (C). The thread that was taped out of the way in the beginning is now untaped and wound in spiral fashion over the just-completed basic underwrap (D). The end of the spiraled thread is anchored underneath a narrow trim band at the other end of the wrap (E).

Guide wrap with tied-under spirals.

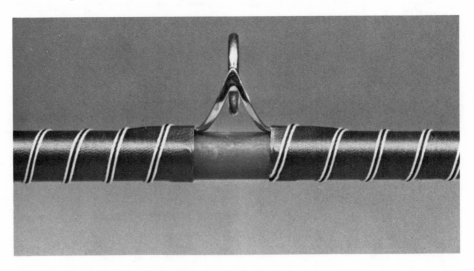

Butt wrap with tied-under spiral.

Good wrapping technique requires patience and practice to learn. Master the basic wraps before you attempt the more complicated patterns. Rod wrapping thread is inexpensive, so do not hesitate to do a wrap over when you are dissatisfied with your result. As you progress, you must be willing to experiment if you are to become skillful and original. On the other hand, if you are patient and work carefully, always planning ahead, you will be surprised how easily intricate rod wrapping can be mastered.

FINAL STEPS AND FINISHING

Before you apply the color preserver and protective coating, take a few minutes to inspect each wrap. Make sure no threads climbed on top of previous windings. If you find these, you may be able to work them down into position with your thumbnail, but you probably will have to replace the wrap. Similarly, check to make sure that all the wraps are tight with no space showing through. If pressure from your thumbnail will not close any spaces, try pushing against the wrap with the dull back edge of a knife. Square off the edges of all narrow trim bands with your thumbnail while rotating the rod.

All thread ends should have been cut off as close as possible with a sharp razor blade or X-Acto knife. However, winding thread is made of very thin fibers twisted together, and some of these fibers may have frayed when the thread was cut. At this stage they may appear as occasional fine fuzz. However, when the protective coating is applied, they form tiny hard spots that stick out from the wrappings and detract from the desired glasslike finish. One way to eliminate them is to carefully singe each such spot with a flame. Obviously, you will burn and damage the wraps if you hold them in the flame too long. A very quick pass with the flame is all that is needed. If you decide to singe any protruding cut ends, lower the match from above briefly onto the flaw. Do *not* pass the rod over the flame. Soot and carbon travel up from the flame and will be deposited on your wrappings.

COLOR PRESERVATIVE

To preserve the colors of your wrapping thread and eliminate any blotches, it is necessary to use color preservative. This is a clear plastic lacquer the consistency of water. It needs to be quite thin to penetrate the wrappings. While it can be applied with a brush, you will do better with your index finger, since you can then work it into the wrappings. Dip the tip of your index finger into the bottle, touch your thumb, and roll the wrappings between finger and thumb. Make sure each wrap receives a thorough coat, especially in the crevices around guides. The preservative dries rapidly, so as soon as the original color returns you can give the wraps the second coat. Two or three coats are required.

Color preserver is applied with the fingers.

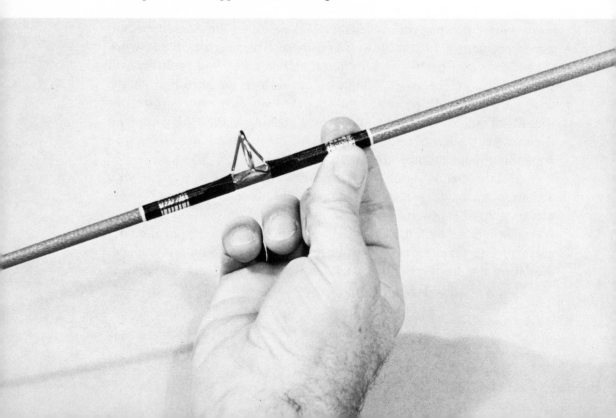

SIGNATURE

Every custom rod builder is proud of the rod he himself has designed and assembled. Nothing speaks so clearly of that pride and craftsmanship as the builder's signature written on the rod. On my own rods, I simply sign my name. On rods built for gifts, I write "Custom built for (whoever) by Dale Clemens." This is written in three lines around the blank just above the hookkeeper. Use India ink and a fine-point drawing pen. Use a light pressure on the pen—only enough to cause the ink to flow.

Signature on my personal rods.

The form I use when making a rod for someone else. A third line, not visible, reads "by Dale P. Clemens."

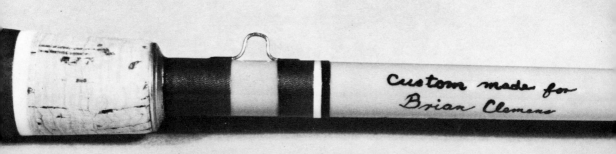

Since it is a bit tricky writing on a curved polished surface, keep a damp rag or paper tissue handy. If you make a mistake, it is an easy matter to quickly wipe off the blank and start over. If you can't get the hang of it, use steel wool or very fine sandpaper to gently dull the polished surface of the blank. When the ink is completely dry, coat the signature with varnish to prevent it from rubbing off. This will also restore the luster to the blank if you find it necessary to dull the polished surface.

PROTECTIVE FINISH

The traditional finish for wrappings has been varnish, since it provides a tough, clear finish. When a brush is used, air bubbles are frequently formed. You will never end up with the desired smooth finish as long as these bubbles are present. It seems the harder you work with a brush to eliminate bubbles in varnish, the more they form. For this reason, the good old index finger is again your best tool. Varnishing the entire rod is not necessary, since quality fiberglass blanks are treated with a final coat of special resin which seals and provides a smooth glasslike finish. Cover only all of the wrappings (and your signature). Apply two to three thin coats, allowing adequate drying time

Applying an epoxy protective finish to the wraps.

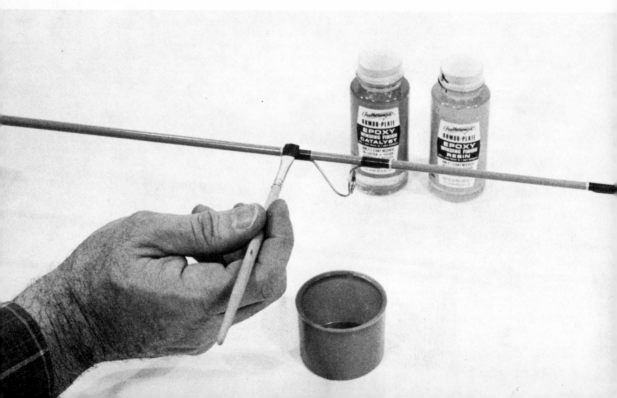

(generally twenty-four hours) between coats. Since varnish dries slowly, set the rod aside in a dust-free place while each coat dries.

In recent years, an aerosol-spray rod finish has come on the market that can be used instead of varnish for coating the wrappings. In trying it, I found it does provide a good tough finish, but that it requires a lot more work and care to apply. In order to keep the spray off guides, ferrules, and grip, these must be masked. It is a laborious job to mask off each guide so that the metal is covered with masking tape but the spray will still reach all parts of the wrappings. The manufacturer of the brand I used suggested coating the metal guides with vaseline as an alternative to masking tape. This sounded pretty messy to me and I felt it would be difficult to remove it later without getting it all over the rod. Five light coats are recommended, and if you are unfamiliar with spraying techniques, there is a lot of opportunity to get unsightly runs and sags in the finish. These develop rather easily on a round surface such as a fishing rod. To eliminate them, move the spray can absolutely parallel with the surface of the rod over its entire length, and at a steady speed. The speed of your pass should be fairly rapid—and never pause for even an instant. Rotate the rod about 120° after each pass so that you will cover the rod in three passes, each slightly overlapping the other. It can, of course, be done successfully, and will provide an attractive, durable finish over the entire rod. However, that presents another problem for light rods, since a coating over the entire blank tends to stiffen the action somewhat. Perhaps the best use of the aerosol rod finish is for refinishing old rods. In building new rods, I'll stick to the simple varnish-and-index-finger method or to one of the finishes discussed below.

A clear epoxy finish is now available that provides a very strong covering for wrappings. This is made in two solutions (resin and hardener), which are mixed together. It cures, or dries, by catalytic action. Do not confuse this with epoxy glue, which is much too thick to apply over wraps. The desired finish is more like a clear paint or varnish. Unfortunately, not many tackle dealers carry this product yet, and your best source will be hobby stores. It must be applied with a brush, so be sure to purchase some thinner if you want to be able to clean and use the brush again.

Some rod builders use clear fiberglass resin for covering their wraps. This also cures by catalytic action, and a small amount of hardener must be mixed with it just before using. The finish it provides is good in all respects. Its greatest drawback is that it is available only in large sizes—quarts and sometimes pints. The hardener for that quantity is only an ounce or two, so that it is rather difficult to properly mix the small amounts needed for coating rod wraps. If you decide to try it, your best source of supply is boat dealers who sell it for fiberglassing boats.

Both epoxy and fiberglass resin must be applied with a brush. You will need a quality flat brush about ½ inch wide, preferably of sable. Support the rod section at two points so that the rod can be rotated under the brush. Work with the brush fairly full of the solution, and flow it onto the wraps—but not so thickly that sags develop. Once you have touched the brush to the wraps, try not to lift it from the work. Spread the solution onto the wraps by rotating the rod while you move the brush slowly along the length of the wrap. Make sure your finish extends about ⅛ inch beyond the edge of each wrap so as to fully protect it.

When you have coated all the wraps, set the rod aside in a dust-free place until the finish has completely cured. With fiberglass resin, plan on two coats. With epoxy, you will need at least two coats. Consult the directions on the container to be sure.

MAKING A ROD-WINDING JIG

The rod-winding jig mentioned earlier in this chapter can be easily made and will find other uses than just winding on wraps. It is an excellent support for quite a few different rod-building operations, as you will discover once you have one. With it you will be able to wrap guides and apply the protective coating more rapidly than by any other method.

The heart of the jig is two or three blocks of wood that can be slid along a wood rail. On each of these blocks, two inexpensive plastic casters are mounted upside down, with their wheels barely touching. The rod is cradled in this junction of the caster wheels and can therefore be revolved easily.

A second wood rail is fastened to the workbench 6 inches to 12 inches behind, and parallel to, the first rail. On it slides one wood

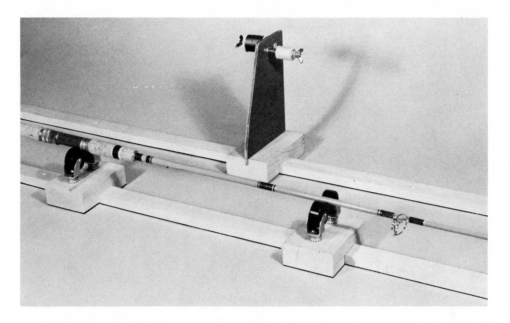

A homemade winding jig. The blocks on which the casters are mounted slide along the front rail, and the block that holds the spool arbors slides on the rear rail. Thread tension is adjusted with the wingnuts.

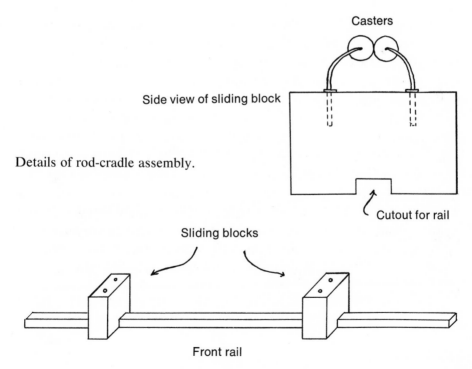

Casters

Side view of sliding block

Details of rod-cradle assembly.

Cutout for rail

Sliding blocks

Front rail

175

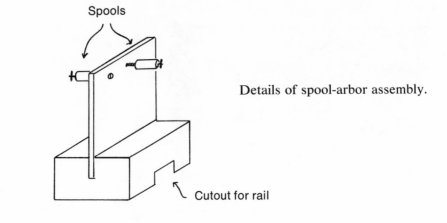

Spools

Details of spool-arbor assembly.

Cutout for rail

Spring   Wingnut

Spool

Washers

block. This block is fitted with a piece of plywood which stands vertically and at a right angle to the rail. The height of the piece of plywood is sufficient to place the top a few inches higher than the junction of the caster wheels on the front rail blocks. Two holes are drilled through the plywood near the top, and a bolt long enough to hold a spool of rod-winding thread is inserted through each hole—one to the right and one to the left. A nut is tightened on the bolt against the other side of the plywood to anchor the bolt in position. Next, onto the bolt is placed a metal washer, a spring, another metal washer, the spool of rod-winding thread, another metal washer, and finally a thumbscrew. Thread tension is adjusted by tightening the thumbscrew and nut. Spools of thread can be removed and changed easily. However, always make sure the spools are positioned so that the thread comes from the top on the spool on your left and from underneath on the spool on your right.

176

The accompanying diagrams may make it easier to visualize the assembly. No dimensions are given because absolutely none are critical in any way. Scrap lumber can be used for all wood parts. For example, my blocks holding the casters and the plywood support for the thread were all made from lengths of two-by-fours. My rails are lengths of one-by-twos. Just make sure the rails are parallel, and that the blocks holding the casters are all the same height. Finishing is unnecessary, except to sand rough edges which could be a source of splinters.

Your local hardware store can supply the few pieces of hardware required. The size of the casters does not matter as long as they are all the same. They can be of the type that is mounted on a shaft, which you will insert in a drilled hole of the proper size. Or they can be of the type mounted on a plate, which you will screw to the wood blocks. They can be quite light and inexpensive, since they will support only the weight of a rod. Their cost will probably be about 25¢ to 50¢ each.

All the wood blocks simply sit on top of the rail and can be easily removed for storage. If your workbench must also be used for other projects, the rails can be attached with a few countersunk screws, enabling the rails to be removed too. The sheet of plywood holding the spools of thread can be attached to the base block with right-angle metal brackets, or glued into a slit, or saw kerf, cut part way into the base block. The important thing is the basic concept of the jig. Your own ideas on construction can be utilized.

The jig is a pleasure to use. Since the casters cradle the rod, you are relieved of holding it. One hand can rotate the rod while the other guides the thread into position and adjusts tension as the thread passes through thumb and forefinger. Temporary extra tension can also be applied by cupping a hand over the spool. When making long underwraps of one continuous color, lay the bottom of your open palm across the rod. By moving your palm down and toward you, you can effect a number of complete revolutions more rapidly and more easily than by turning the rod with thumb and forefinger. For special effects, you can even wind two colors of thread simultaneously. To do this, bring the two threads together between your thumb and forefinger just above the rod. Use this hand to guide the threads onto the rod while you rotate it with the other hand.

8. Rod Care

Now that you have made that "one-of-a-kind" rod, your skill and craftsmanship should be protected to the fullest. Your pride will dictate that you give it the good care to which it is entitled. If you treat your rod well, it will give you a lifetime of the most enjoyable fishing.

Cloth bag

A soft compartmented cloth bag, for inside your rod case, will do much to protect the rod against scratching and marring. It will keep the sections from rubbing directly against each other, and will cushion them inside the rod case. Flannelette or corduroy are both excellent, but any good-quality soft cloth will do just fine.

Since the construction of a cloth case is so simple, anyone who knows her way around a sewing machine can easily make one for you. If that someone happens to be your wife, she already may have adequate scraps of material. If you plan on building a number of rods over the years, give thought to purchasing a piece of cloth from which identical rod bags can be made. A piece of cloth two yards or a little less in length will be more than adequate to handle the longest section of a rod. It generally comes in 45-inch widths—which will make many bags. Corduroy sells for about $2 a running yard and flannelette for about 60¢. So the cost spread over a number of rods is negligible for matching custom rod bags. Corduroy is available in a wide range of solid colors and flannelette in a great array of patterns—including little duckies and fire engines, since one of its main uses is for children's pajamas. It *is* a custom rod, and all along I've encouraged you to do your own thing, so – maybe you really want to have something different!

As mentioned, the construction is quite easy: a long narrow bag, stitched on the wrong side, then turned inside out, with a seam dividing it off center into two pockets. The open end has a short flap to which is stitched a length of twill tape for tying. When working out the measurements, be sure to make the pockets wide enough to hold the grip and the wide butt guide on spinning rods. If you want to personalize the bag, write your name on a piece of iron-on tape with a ball-point pen or fabric-marking pen, then place it near the top of the bag. I do this on rods I make for gifts to add that little extra touch. On my own bags, I mark the particular model of the rod on the tape, since I frequently travel with a number of rods in one large travel case. This makes it easier to select the particular rod I want. I'll confess that it also makes it simpler to match up the mess of bags and rods strewn around the room at the end of a week's fishing.

Rod case

By all means keep your rod in a hard protective case. More rods have been damaged in transit or around the house than were ever broken while fishing. In purchasing a case, you have a wide variety from which to choose: aluminum, plastic, or cardboard, and fixed-length or adjustable. I have bought some very nice, yet quite inexpensive ones from among the collection of odd cases that sporting goods dealers seem to accumulate over the years from their display rods.

Don't overlook the possibility of making your own. Some of my first cases were made from the heavy cardboard tubes that carpeting is rolled around. They generally were about 2½ inches outside diameter with ¼-inch-thick walls. I fitted a wooden disk for the bottom and glued it into position. For the top I beveled the outside edge of the tube to make it easy to slip the end cap on and off. The end cap was simply a discarded top, of the right size, from the various aerosol spray cans so much in use. The outside of the case was sealed with a few coats of shellac and then painted. They cost me next to nothing, and are still quite serviceable.

A great material available today for home-crafted cases is the plastic pipe used in plumbing. It comes in various diameters with matching end caps, is light, and very strong. If desired, it can be painted. I told a friend about this a year ago, and on a recent trip he arrived at the airport with a number of these cases taped securely together. He had even taped on a carrying handle with the end result of a very serviceable and strong case ideally suited to the rigors of today's airline travel.

Whatever your case, it is a good idea to mark your name and address on the outside. This can be done with a label, pen and ink, or paint. Cover this with a coat of clear varnish or lacquer for durability.

Care of rod

Today's fiberglass rods do not require nearly the painstaking care that bamboo needs. But don't ignore your rod. A few simple steps will keep it looking like new for years. When you finish fishing in fresh water, always take a minute to wipe the rod before putting it away. If you have been fishing in salt water, wash it down with fresh water, using soap occasionally. I have done a fair amount of light-tackle salt-water fishing, and for years I have had the habit of taking my disassembled rod and reel with me into the shower at the end of the day. When finished, I run a towel over the rod and let it stand in a corner overnight to air-dry. As a result, I have rarely had to refinish a rod, and my guides do not show the telltale greenish marks of saltwater corrosion. Normally, that is all the cleaning my rods ever get or need. The one exception is the cork grips, which are bound to soil and darken after a lot of hard use. However, soiled grips can be restored to an almost-new appearance by a thorough scrubbing with a soap-filled steel wool pad, such as Brillo. Wooden handles of trolling rods will, in time, need to be sanded and new varnish applied. Wood ring inserts in the grip need to be rubbed occasionally with a few drops of boiled linseed oil, or revarnished.

Periodic inspection will eliminate some serious problems before they occur. Frequently check the tip-top and other guides for grooving from monofilament lines. Even the slightest indication of a groove means it's time to replace the tip-top or the guide. If not, your line will fray and weaken and seriously impair your chances of landing a fish.

While casting, if you ever notice a rocking effect at the ferrule, stop fishing. If this is not repaired right away, you stand a very good chance of snapping the rod. If you catch it soon enough, the only repair needed may be to recement the ferrule in place. If there is evidence of more serious wear, you probably need to replace the ferrule.

The best fishing occurs at the out-of-the-way locations where it is impossible to secure replacement parts if something does go wrong. For this reason, I always carry a small simple repair kit in my tackle box. It includes a few spare tip-tops in different sizes, stick ferrule cement, a few assorted guides, a small spool of wrapping thread, and a razor blade. All of it fits into a small plastic box that some forgotten lure came in. It has saved the day—or a whole week's trip—on a number of occasions for me or a fishing friend. There is no need to be fancy in these circumstances, just serviceable. The wrong-size guide or tip-top, pressed into service, will allow you to continue fishing until you get home and make the proper repairs.

TRAVEL

Modern highways, jet planes, and increased leisure time have been a boon to fishermen everywhere. Some of the places I only dreamed about twenty years ago are among my fishing grounds today. As each year passes, the truly good fishing is farther afield. So for many of us, fishing now and in the future means becoming a wide-ranging traveler.

I have already stressed the need to use a durable rod case and cloth bag. This provides adequate protection for storage and the short trip to the nearby lake. However, extra care is called for on longer jaunts, especially if you travel by air. Rough baggage handling has always plagued travelers, but the jet plane has introduced us to a new problem—vibration. To give you an idea of how serious this can be, professional photographers have found that the cemented glass elements of their lenses will loosen from much air travel. These expensive optics are perfectly fitted and bonded together with the most modern adhesives, yet they weaken when exposed to the constant vibration from a jet plane. Seemingly indestructible fiberglass fishing rods, impervious to moisture and capable of being bent practically double, find one of their worst enemies in vibration. This was pointed out recently by Phil Clock, President of Fenwick/Sevenstrand, in an article he wrote for the *Fenwick Newsletter.* So if you are going to protect your investment and your craftsmanship, special packing will be necessary for air travel.

Fortunately, an inexpensive material, soft plastic foam (or foam rubber), provides excellent protection from vibration, as well as cushioning the hard knocks we must expect. Business and industry use soft plastic foam widely as a packing material. So the next time you unpack something, check — you just may find a bonus. Many of the office supplies we receive are packed with sheets or pieces of soft plastic foam, and our office girls always save them for me. With a little ingenuity I am sure you can come up with a similar free source, since you will need only a few pieces.

Using the foam to protect your rod in its case is easy. First, cut a few circular pieces to fit into the bottom and top of the case. These can either be dropped loosely into place or can be attached with a daub of glue. At two or three places along the length of the rod, wrap a 2-to-3-inch-wide strip of foam around the rod in its cloth bag. These can be held in place with either rubber bands or "twist-on" paper-covered wire. The rod with its foam girdles is then slipped into the hard case.

While I have individual cases for each of my rods, I use only one large-diameter whalebone plastic rod case for airline travel. The length is adjustable and it is big enough to hold quite a few rods. Each rod is first placed in its individual cloth bag. The rods are then arranged in a tight-fitting vertical bundle with all the tips pointing up. A 2-to-3-inch-wide strip of foam is wrapped around the bottom and again at the middle. Since the rods are of different lengths, the fragile tips come to various heights in the bundle. Each of these needs extra padding, so a foam strip is used at each of these points. To further protect the tip on the longest rod at the top of the stack, a strip of foam is doubled over the end. The whole bundle is then slipped into the rod case, and should fit snugly. If not, a few additional pieces of foam are used.

Incidentally, the sheets of foam have other excellent uses in packing for fishing trips. Your tackle box will probably contain reels, lures, and all those miscellaneous little items we find so necessary to our sport. As long as you carry the box upright by the handle, everything will remain in its assigned place.

I am convinced, however, that airline baggage handlers will, in the course of a trip, put your box in every conceivable position: on end,

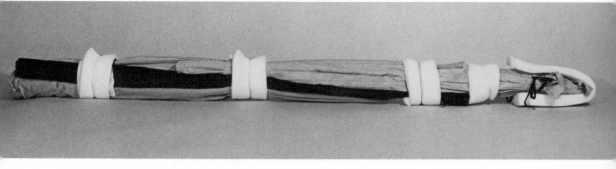

To pack rods for travel, a number of rods, each in its cloth bag, are arranged together. Strips of soft plastic foam girdle the package and cushion the rod tips.

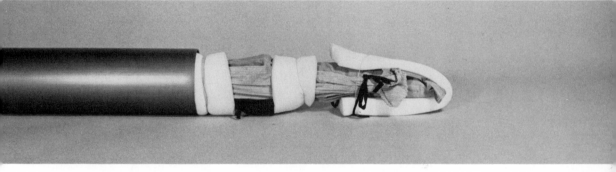

Rod bundle is inserted in bottom half of a large tube.

Closed case ready for the baggage hold. Label contains name and address and is varnished for protection.

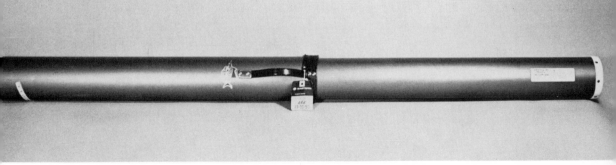

upside down, and on its side. The resulting snarl of hooks, swivels, etc. can put a jigsaw puzzle to shame. For this reason, I cut small rectangles of foam to fit over those compartments that contain all the loose small parts, effectively keeping them in place no matter what diabolical gyrations the box is put through.

In the bottom of the box I pack reels and fragile plastic boxes in pieces of foam. If the contents do not completely fill that section, I lay foam sheets on top. Then, when the bottom tray comes down into position, everything is tight and cushioned. Soft plastic foam is really the traveling fisherman's best friend.

Appendix:
Retail mail
order companies

Since most rod builders will find it necessary to purchase blanks and components through the mail, I have listed those retail mail order companies that I know of at the present. I am sure this list is not conclusive, and to those I missed I apologize. The merchandise sold by these firms now varies greatly. Some carry only certain types of blanks (fly, casting, etc.) that meet popular demand in their particular geographic area. Others carry only kits and a few components. Finally some carry a very broad and complete line of both blanks and components. While I would like to provide the reader with a better indication of who carries what, it would be difficult and unfair, because the interest in custom-rod building is growing so rapidly that the merchandise these firms stock is changing from year to year. For the names of other companies entering the field in the future, I would suggest you check the classified sections of the various outdoor magazines.

Angler's Pro Shop, Box 35, Springfield, Ohio 45501
Cabela's Inc., P.O. Box 199, 812 13th Avenue, Sidney, Nebraska 69162
Dale Clemens Custom Tackle, Box 415, Route 3, Allentown, Pa. 18104
Coren's Rod & Reel Service, 6532 North Clark St., Chicago, Illinois 60626
J. Lee Cuddy Associates, Inc., 450 N.E. 79th St., Miami, Florida 33138
Jack Dickerson's Inc., Box 172, Camden, Missouri 65020

Finnysports, 2910 Glanzman Rd., Toledo, Ohio 43614

Fireside Angler, Box 823, Melville, New York 11746

Herter's Inc., Waseca, Minnesota 56093

E. Hille, 815 Railway Street, Box 269, Williamsport, Pa. 17701

Limit Manufacturing Corporation, 515 Melody Lane, Richardson, Texas 75080

Midland Tackle Company, Route 17, Sloatsburg, New York 10974

Netcraft Company, 3101 Sylvania Avenue, Toledo, Ohio 43613

Okie Bug, 3501 South Sheridan, Tulsa, Oklahoma 74145

Orvis Company, Inc., Manchester, Vermont 05254

Rangeley Region Sports Shop, 28 Main Street, Rangeley, Maine 04970

Reed Tackle, Box 390, Caldwell, New Jersey 07006

Index

INDEX